HUMAN RIGHTS
AND THE USES
OF HISTORY

HUMAN RIGHTS AND THE USES OF HISTORY

SAMUEL MOYN

VERSO
London • New York

First published by Verso 2014
© Samuel Moyn 2014

1 3 5 7 9 10 8 6 4 2

Verso
UK: 6 Meard Street, London W1F 0EG
US: 20 Jay Street, Suite 1010, Brooklyn, NY 11201
www.versobooks.com

Verso is the imprint of New Left Books

ISBN-13: 978-1-78168-263-0
eISBN-13: 978-1-78168-264-7 (US)
eISBN-13: 978-1-78168-652-2 (UK)

British Library Cataloguing in Publication Data
A catalogue record for this book is available from the British Library

Library of Congress Cataloging-in-Publication Data
A catalog record for this book is available from the Library of Congress

Typeset in Sabon by Hewer Text UK Ltd, Edinburgh, Scotland
Printed in the US by Maple Press

For Sara and her new family

If one would like to see our European morality for once as it looks from a distance, and if one would like to measure it against other moralities, past and future, then one has to proceed like a traveler who wants to know how high the towers in a town are: he *leaves* the city.

—Friedrich Nietzsche

Spartam nactus es; hanc exorna (The city of Sparta is your portion; now embellish her) ... A man full of warm, speculative benevolence may wish his society otherwise constituted than he finds it; but a good patriot, and a true politician, always considers how he shall make the most of the existing materials ... There is something else than the mere alternative of absolute destruction, or unreformed existence.

—Edmund Burke

CONTENTS

PREFACE

All history is contemporary history, Benedetto Croce said, and nowhere is this maxim truer than when it comes to the sudden rise of human rights history. A few short years ago, there was no such domain of historical inquiry. Now it is ubiquitous. It has verged on absorbing past themes that once stood on their own or served other purposes, like the meaning of the eighteenth-century Atlantic revolutions or the nineteenth-century campaigns against slavery. And it has sparked new and fascinating investigations into transformations of world governance, social movements, and international law.

And yet the rise of human rights history raises plenty of questions of its own. This sequence of essays presents my engagements with other attempts to stake out the coordinates of the domain. It was these inquiries into how others proposed to define a new field that originally drove me on the path to my own interpretation of where human rights came from, which appeared as *The Last Utopia*[1] a few years ago—and which I am now follow-

---

1. Samuel Moyn, *The Last Utopia: Human Rights in History* (Cambridge, MA, 2010).

ing towards a sequel on contemporary developments. The emphasis of these essays falls on distinguishing the abuses from the uses of history for thinking about the present and future of one of the most central notions and most illustrious political movements of our time.

Historians always engage in a double activity, beyond the accumulation of information that provides the necessary basis of their work. One is to demonstrate that facts about the past, even new facts, do not compel interpretations, which are always inflected by our own circumstances. And in particular, anxious about the threat of anachronism our present-day perspective necessarily breeds, historians show how other views, usually through selective evidence or misleading interpretation, betray the dead whom the writing of history is supposed to let live again on their own terms.

In this sense, history should be "antiquarian." Insofar as they are not ideologues, historians think that, whatever the ethical value of the past, there is also an ethical command to respect its "alterity." They feel the power of Jacob Burckhardt's moral outrage at those who cast the annals as no more than a vast preparation for the way things are, and the way people think, right now: "Each man regards all times as fulfilled in his own, and cannot see his own as one of many passing waves. Just as if the world and its history had existed merely for our sakes!"[2] Our ancestors were trying to be themselves rather than to anticipate somebody else. The past is not simply a mirror for our own self-regard.

And yet antiquarianism for its own sake is neither viable nor desirable. Too little understood is that arguments about history—including arguments insisting on

---

2. Jacob Burckhardt, *Force and Freedom: Reflections on History*, translated by James Hastings Nichols (New York, 1943), p. 358.

the autonomy of the past from the present—can never do other than serve the present, since they are inevitably motivated by its chronologically temporary and thematically narrow concerns.[3] The stress on the different futures the past left open only takes place in the mix of a broader and undoubtedly presentist activity, that either monumentalizes some current person, group, or project, or criticizes them in the name of something different. Whatever respect we owe the dead, history is still written by—and meaningful to—the living. If so, abuses of the past call for uses in the name of a better future.

In the old days, when Burckhardt's companion Friedrich Nietzsche originally offered the distinction between antiquarian, monumental, and critical history, it was the nation-state that historians chose to build up or tear down; in our day, it has frequently become human rights, along with their international laws and transnational servants. The main goal of this book is to insist on the critical impulse: human rights history should turn away from ransacking the past as if it provided good support for the astonishingly specific international movement of the last few decades. That movement comprises a politics for which history offers little validation because it is so new. If study of the past is useful at all in coming to terms with what happens today in the name of timeless and universal values, it suggests the reinvention of our movement in the name of a more just world. Human rights have so far done too little to bring that world about, which leaves a task beyond interpreting the past: crafting the future.

These chapters make particularly vivid the intersection of the writing of human rights history with America's

---

3. Compare Quentin Skinner, *Visions of Politics*, 3 vols. (Cambridge, 2001).

politics of liberal internationalism, which rose after the horrors of the Vietnam War in tandem with the search for a new geopolitical role for the country. Invented just before the end of the Cold War, liberal internationalism surged in the decade after, with massive consequences for history. The search for the origins of human rights is a by-product of the end of the Cold War—more specifically, the temporary age between the bipolar standoff of the past and the multipolar struggle of the future. During what now seems a brief post–Cold War interregnum that will not last long, human rights looked to a great many like a concept that could bridge the distance between unipolarity and humanity itself. If there is a common thread in what follows, it is that liberal internationalism has both motivated and misled our inevitable conversation with the past about what to think and how to proceed now—not least because America's unipolar moment seems set to wane. The history of human rights first emerged as something like the history of American morals, analogous to texts that Victorians once wrote to assess how far they had come and to stabilize the self-regard of their civilization even as the threats began to lurk that would soon engulf them in catastrophe and decline. Now it looks like the confused early epitaph of a giant entering senescence.

The evidence from the past for the centrality of human rights to the new liberal internationalism is hardly promising. The ancient past from the Greeks and the Bible on hardly provided plausible sources, but then it has always been easy to update the myth of "Western civilization" to suit momentary agendas. The Atlantic revolutions did not serve much better, notwithstanding President Jimmy Carter's rousing assertion in his farewell address to the country: "America did not invent human rights," he noted, introducing a theme repeated in variation by every president since. "In a very real sense, it is the other way round. Human rights invented America."[4] Yet especially in the origins of America (not to mention France), rights had originally been a revolutionary conception, authorizing violence if necessary, and for the sake of national liberation. In the recent search for a usable past under the auspices of America's liberal internationalism, however, the revolutionary origins of rights have been domesticated and the primarily statist and nationalist associations rights maintained for most of modern history were quietly dropped. The first chapter of this collection, on the book by Lynn Hunt on the revolutionary origins of human rights that has done most to define the field, pursues these troubling reinventions.

Worse yet, the British empire against which American revolutionary rights were originally asserted became a prized source for the new human rights history in the age of American liberal internationalism—and perhaps not surprisingly, since Great Britain did have its own early version of liberal internationalism, corrupted though it was by formal imperialism. In fact, humanitarianism and rights rarely crossed into (let alone defined) each other in the hierarchical global order and world visions of the nineteenth century. But an imperial rhetoric of fellow-feeling benevolence sometimes associated with Great Britain's global preeminence has been explicitly revived in human rights history as template and threat. On the one hand, it is a model in which uplifting moralizing seems often taken at face value—as if the British Empire's leading role in combating the slave trade or targeting other people's violence in early humanitarian intervention were worth dusting

---

4. Jimmy Carter, "Farewell Address," January 14, 1981.

off now, without reflecting on their congenital impurity first. On the other, it is a hazard in which Britain's high-minded excuses for violent rulership show why its record has to be treated as a cautionary tale that the less self-interested and more authentically humane American hegemony will avoid.

Several of the chapters consider the British Empire as a source of human rights and a comparative template for liberal internationalism today. I reach the position that it is misleading to treat the British imperial past as a museum of horrors from which a few masterpieces are to be salvaged today to mount on our own walls. In part, the reason is that it is wrong to regard writing history as a project of moral connoisseurship allowing past enterprises to be saved from their own times. But in part, the reason is that there is no absolute way to distinguish between their maleficent empire and our benevolent hegemony; and if so, our desire to admire the good parts of a past we otherwise abhor in order to smuggle them across a neatly marked border can never be fulfilled. There is little interest in unmasking liberal internationalism as an imperialism that dare not speak its name. But by the same token, the relationship between the past and present is far too murky to allow simple reclamation of its good things, while exempting ourselves from its abhorrent violence.

Not all Americans are liberal internationalists, and it would clearly be wrong to reduce the uses and abuses of history within the field of human rights to this framework. And I am myself of course subject to the maxim that all history is contemporary history. Reviewing these chapters, it is clear to me how deeply I have responded, in the years since the search for the origins of human rights began, to a specifically American vision of liberal internationalism that the end of the Cold War seemed to anoint as the framework for a human global order in the future. When I criticize others for keeping that dream alive rather than reflecting on the consequences of our experiences—notably but not exclusively in the Iraq war—for our original assumptions, I am clearly writing from a time-bound and local resistance to a central item in recent American intellectual history. More to the point, I am engaging as much in self-criticism as anything else, for few avoided the enthusiasm that the post–Cold War moment evoked through the dream of human rights.

That is why, unlike some harsher critics of human rights, I strive in this book to understand what made humanitarianism for Great Britain and human rights for the United States much more than rhetorics of global engagement. For one thing, neither country's representatives could claim proprietary control over them, which could serve and have served to indict them and their projects as much as to serve those projects.

If those who invoke humanity always and simply are trying to cheat for the sake of narrow interests, as the great (though Nazi) jurist Carl Schmitt famously alleged, it would not explain why anyone ever believes in them, or why the regular response to ideological mobilizations of sentimental and ethical norms is new and sometimes more generous claims on human universalism. This book cynically punctures illusions, historical and political, but not in the name of cynicism. If humanitarianism had been purely rhetorical high-mindedness for Britain, or human rights were simply an apology for American power, they would never have become the highly mobile and contested categories they remain today.

For that reason, I have sought in and through historical commentary and scholarship to understand not simply the conditions in which human rights could play the role of post–Cold War creed for liberal internationalists but also how they might transcend that role. To do so, the specific historical role international human rights have taken on needs to be grasped—a project ill-served by associating them with violent revolution or imperialist humanitarianism. Not that there is no continuity in history, but these old projects do not repay the study they have attracted in the search for the origins of our highest moral beliefs and aspirational legal projects.

Instead, my argument insists on the need to look in a more recent time for the inception of international human rights politics. A last tranche of these essays touches on a contrast I have pursued at much greater length in *The Last Utopia*: between the 1940s when human rights fell on deaf ears, and the 1970s when they experienced their first global breakthrough. A summary piece presents my general reasoning in this regard. It bears the marks of the moment it was published, under Barack Obama's first term as president and his decision (surprising and disappointing to some fervent enthusiasts) to give human rights norms a back seat as the global struggle against terrorism continued, albeit with some modest tweaks.

Given the risk of occluding the important fact that America in the 1970s came a few years late to the cause of universal human rights, especially at the level of social movements, a subsequent piece emphasizes how Amnesty International—at first a British and West European group—paved the way for the global anti-torture norm so much at play in recent American political debates. But America like the entirety of the transatlantic space (including once-Communist lands after the Cold War ended) was the scene of a vigorous reconceptualization of World War II several decades after the fact. In fact, it is broadly mistaken to associate human rights in their era of annunciation with Holocaust consciousness, of which there was little for a long time. But surely the next item on the agenda is to conceptualize and research their intersection, which fatefully affected both.

Culminating in the 1970s, these essays do not give a fair sense of the global radiance of human rights in our times, in considerably different forms, and especially their role in European governance. An epilogue reconsiders the argument, offering some reasons to reclaim human rights from the liberal internationalism that has as much neutralized their implications—especially when it comes to economic and social rights—as accounted for their fame. In my judgment, the history of rights in domestic spaces offers considerable material for reflection on how to push human rights beyond their accommodating version in recent history. If human rights originated in our time as a response to the perceived failures of nationalism and socialism, at first for the sake of a minimalist reform (though ending up serving as a core theme of post–Cold War rhetoric), it will take spirit and energy to push them in a new direction. There is no historical basis in international affairs for this program, but the history of rights as citizenship entitlements so profoundly redefined through vision and contest offers a memorable basis for the future.

In domestic spaces, rights as formal entitlements concerning mind and body were not only given further enumeration to honor the claims of the least powerful, but were placed within a social vision authorizing the state to seek the conditions for citizen enjoyment of entitlements of all sorts. Any new human rights movement will, to be sure, need to be different, not least in ensuring that local and global politics intersect in ways that the older progressive movement failed to imagine, let alone accomplish. To use the past in a better way than to abuse it for the sake of the limited human rights movement of our day, with its post–Cold War dreams and disappointing outcomes, seems the most worthwhile goal.

ON THE GENEALOGY OF MORALS

The enterprise of writing the history of human rights has become a widespread activity only in the past decade. Lynn Hunt's *Inventing Human Rights* is its most prominent result so far, identifying the Enlightenment and the age of democratic revolutions as the moment when the cause was born.[1] Yet if human rights history is now chic, it is also confused. Not long ago the president of the main American professional association of historians announced to all students of the past—whatever the place and time and subject of their research—that they "are all historians of human rights."[2] But what could such a claim possibly mean?

The most troubling shortcoming of the contemporary attempt to give human rights a history is that it distorts the past to suit the present. And in this gambit, it is late, fatally late: the current wave of human rights history is the tardy fruit of the fashion of human rights in politics, and contributors to the genre clearly set out to provide

---

1. Lynn Hunt, *Inventing Human Rights: A History* (New York, 2007).

2. Linda K. Kerber, "We Are All Historians of Human Rights," *Perspectives: Newsmagazine of the American Historical Association* 44, no. 7 (October 2006): 3–4.

backstories to the vogue of human rights just a few years ago, when they exercised a literally millennial appeal. But the vine withered as the fruit ripened. The sad fact is that historiography has not caught up with history, and even the professionals—especially the professionals—are still providing the prologue to the idealism so powerful during Bill Clinton's presidency.

The shift in political debate has been impossible to miss. Even those who retain an investment in human rights cannot treat them as an unquestionable good, mainly because the America that once seemed to many enthusiasts to be the prospective servant of universality abroad all too quickly became the America pursuing low-minded imperial ambitions in high-minded human-itarian tones. The effect on human rights as a public language and political cause has been staggering, and it is not yet clear whether they can recover.

If radical apostasy is the sign that times have changed, then the ideological journey of the writer David Rieff provides the most spectacular evidence. Once a paladin of human rights—and a champion of American humani-tarian intervention—Rieff has now turned on the politics he once embraced. For Rieff, human rights, far from being the universal panacea he and writers such as Michael Ignatieff and Samantha Power once considered them, now stand revealed as an ideology perfectly designed to cloak the "military humanism" of empire.[3] Agree with him or not, Rieff's evolution shows that Communism is not the only god that can fail.

The conversion of Tony Judt has been less radical but more interesting. He made his name excoriating French left-wing intellectuals for their failure to champion

---

3. David Rieff, *At the Point of a Gun: Democratic Dreams and Armed Intervention* (New York, 2006).

rights—a failure he saw as rooted in their nation's revolutionary tradition, especially when measured against Anglo-American political wisdom. Rights have an "extrapolitical status," he wrote thirteen years ago, diagnosing as French pathology the error of making them "an object of suspicion."[4] Now he says that universalistic invocations of rights often mask particular interests—and never more so than in America's current wars—even though he once chastised opponents of rights who took this very position. Formerly treating them as an intellectual talisman, Judt now complains in passing about "the abstract universalism of 'rights'— and uncompromising ethical stands taken against malign regimes in their name." He warns that such abstractions can all too easily lead those who invoke them to "readily mistake the US president's myopic rigidity for their own moral rectitude."[5] Of course, Judt still understands himself to be a committed liberal intellectual, at a time when he thinks practically all other liberals have disappeared. But not just the world has changed; he has too, and most strikingly in his acknowledgment that his old standard can hallow many causes.[6]

The travails of rights today mean there is more, not less, at stake in excavating their history. Hunt's account falls neatly into two parts. The first deals with Enlightenment humanitarianism. She argues that the

---

4. Tony Judt, *Past Imperfect: French Intellectuals, 1944–1956* (Berkeley, 1992), pp. 232–3.

5. Tony Judt, "Bush's Useful Idiots," *London Review of Books,* September 21, 2006, later reprinted in Judt, *Reappraisals: Reflections on the Forgotten Twentieth Century* (New York, 2008), pp. 388–9.

6. Judt responded to these remarks in a letter to the editor of the *Nation,* April 25, 2007, citing one of his favorite tags from John Maynard Keynes: "When the facts change, I change my mind. What do you do?"

early-modern explosion of novels, especially the wildly popular sentimental novels of Samuel Richardson and Jean-Jacques Rousseau, led people beyond aristocratic and religious frameworks to see one another as fellow humans worthy of empathy. In this connection, Hunt devotes an interesting chapter to the eighteenth century's rejection of torture—a topic that gives her book obvious contemporary relevance. Since the majority of human cultures have valued or at least tolerated bodily violation, the repugnance it now inspires has to be explained. Hunt suggests that the rise of sentiment purveyed by the novel combined with a new view of the integrity of the body, with potent results. Torture—together with other corporal violence like honorable dueling, beating wives, spanking children and baiting animals—began to fall from favor in Western culture (save in exported form in colonial rule).[7]

It is true that a rise in compassion for suffering humanity was one ingredient in the explosion of claims for political rights. As Hannah Arendt once observed, in Roman times to call someone a "human" meant referring to him as "outside the range of the law and the body politic of the citizens, as for instance a slave—but certainly a politically irrelevant being."[8] Of course, the eighteenth century had a foundation on which it could build in conferring meaning and value on being human alone. Monotheistic religions always made room for notions of common brotherhood. The source of "empathy" with suffering humanity, for its part, has most plausibly been located in changes in medieval spirituality: Jesus began to be valued as an exemplar of corporal suffering, and Mary became central to Christian piety for having practiced the

---

7. On this murkier—and much later—history of the rise of something like a global anti-torture norm (Hunt's chapter considers only domestic politics), see below, Chapter 7.

8. Hannah Arendt, *On Revolution* (New York, 1963), p. 107.

virtue of compassion.[9] Meanwhile, it is familiar to credit the Renaissance for discovering (or rediscovering) the dignity of man; in his famous study of the Renaissance, Jacob Burckhardt claimed that this period elevated humanity from a merely "logical notion" to a morally resonant force.[10] The eighteenth century doubtless did more to strengthen and secularize the emotive appeals to dignified and suffering humanity than it did to create them. Still, Hunt is surely right about the crucial significance of the Enlightenment—an age of feeling as much as it was an age of reason—for spreading the value of humanity as an end in itself.

If there is a connection between the eighteenth-century rise of humanitarian sentiment and the new wave of rights claims, however, it is only a very loose one. The close relationship Hunt asserts between the two is overly general, because humanitarianism did not and need not always take the form of revolutionary rights assertions or the search for legal guarantees, whether domestic or international. It is also questionable because "rights talk," rooted in ancient Stoicism, Christian natural law and seventeenth-century contractualism, had historical lineages completely different from humanitarianism. The most sensible conclusion to take away from Hunt's book is that the rise of humanitarianism affected and broadened the rights tradition. But it hardly determined it completely.

Hunt links the rise of the phrase "rights of man" in France after the 1750s to the efflorescence of sympathy as a cultural imperative. But, as she shows, the older

---

9. See Rachel Fulton [Brown], *From Judgment to Passion: Devotion to Christ and the Virgin Mary, 800–1200* (New York, 2002), especially Part 2.

10. Jacob Burckhardt, *The Civilization of the Renaissance in Italy*, translated by S. G. C. Middlemore (New York, 1990), p. 229.

language of natural rights persisted, notably in the United States. More important, in spite of her claims that this transformation was also essentially connected with the creation of a new kind of autonomous individual, the humanitarian lineage does not and cannot account for many of the central notions of the rights of man, ones that Hunt ignores: other sorts of judicial guarantees, the right to practice one's religion, the liberty to speak one's mind or publish freely and, above all, the protection of private property.

The second half of Hunt's book turns to some of these subjects, in a highly readable story of the revolutionary declaration of the rights of man. She gives Americans credit for announcing human rights first (even though, again, they used the phrase "natural rights" and did not accord bodily suffering the same centrality). To their discredit, Hunt argues, the Americans did not keep the faith with their own contribution. Luckily, the French soon took up the torch, especially in their Declaration of the Rights of Man and Citizen of 1789. Hunt is most interested in what she repeatedly calls the cascading logic of human rights, whereby those who announced rights were compelled to extend them to Jews, blacks and women (or at least to consider doing so). And when groups initially excluded from humanity were not brought into the fold, as Hunt points out, they sometimes forced the issue. Early feminists like Olympe de Gouges and Mary Wollstonecraft declared the rights of women, while slaves in the French Caribbean demanded liberation.

Even restricting attention to what Hunt does cover, her massively disproportionate emphasis on bodily violation in general and on torture specifically is revealing. Hunt's book is for an audience for whom torture—and other visible state action—is the most grievous affront to morality. But humanitarian sentiment will seem less praiseworthy to anyone who suspects that the focus on visible forms of cruelty obscures structural wrongs that are less easy to see—even when they sometimes also cause the body to suffer, as with the pangs of hunger or the exhaustion of work. This is the sense in which Hunt's narrative is structured to provide background and authority for 1990s humanitarian idealism—and its recent after-effects. There is a relationship between George W. Bush's justification of the Iraq War as a humanitarian campaign against "torture chambers and rape rooms" and the single-minded focus on America's own torture sparked by the Abu Ghraib images.[11] Only very recently could outrage so tightly focused on Abu Ghraib shift to deeper questions, whether about the morality and plausibility of the war and the global relations that permitted it or the inherently violent nature of occupation. Hunt's exclusive concern with spectacular wrongs like torture therefore comes at a price. It leads her to overlook, among other things, the central place held by the right to private property in the declarations of the era, as well as the countervailing pressure for social and economic rights. Strangely, for a book about the revolutionary invention of human rights, Hunt fails even to mention either the "right to work," which first appeared during the French Revolution, or the very different declaration of rights of 1793, which first featured it.

But in the end the main failing of Hunt's book—and the contemporary agenda of human rights history—is not selectivity. In a highly summary concluding chapter, Hunt indicates that the point of her tale is to explain how it later

---

11. See William Saletan, "Rape Rooms: A Chronology," *Slate*, May 5, 2004, slate.com.

became possible for the United Nations to base itself on human rights in its Universal Declaration of Human Rights (1948) and for a global movement to form. But this is to forsake an authentically historical treatment of rights in the age of revolution. And if historians miss how different rights were in the past, they will fail even to recognize what it would take to explain rights in the present.

Hunt often treats "human rights" as a body of ideas somehow insulated from history—as if they were a set of beliefs analogous to heliocentrism or relativity, needing only discovery and acceptance. The protagonists of her book are not people thinking and acting on their convictions but rights themselves, which do things like "creep," "thicken," "gain ground," "gather momentum," "reveal a tendency to cascade," have a "bulldozer force," "make their way ineluctably," "take shape by fits and starts," "take a backseat" and "remain in need of rescue."[12] Hunt provides historical details about the recognition of human rights but ultimately seems to think of them as timeless. In a few mysterious asides, she suggests that rights have biological foundations, in spite of her own demonstration of how chronologically and culturally specific they are.

But a series of interlocking contexts for the revolutionary rights at the center of Hunt's book shows that they need to be differentiated from contemporary "human rights," rather than seen as paving the way for their eventual triumph. So the difficulty is not just that many of the rights of the era are left out of account but that those that are examined need to be put in the proper context.

The first crucial fact is that humanitarianism could underwrite violations of rights as well as their defense. Forty years ago, Arendt argued that the explosion of

---

12. Hunt, *Inventing Human Rights*, pp. 122, 120, 176, 125, 147, 160, 208.

pity was the source not of rights but of terror. The most important text for critically analyzing emotion in the politics of the period, Arendt's *On Revolution* (1963), interpreted Maximilien Robespierre's Terror not as an act of demented criminality but as the first politics based on feeling others' pain. But for Robespierre, the alleviation of suffering required what he called "a compassionate knife" to lance the dangerous pustules on the body politic, purging the enemies of virtue without and within. The results were catastrophic: "*Par pitié, par amour pour l'humanité*," petitioners from the Paris Commune wrote to the National Convention, "*soyez inhumains!*"—out of pity and love of humanity, you must be inhuman.[13] Hunt briefly acknowledges some of the dark sides of a culture of sentimental virtue, like sensationalism and compassion fatigue. But the Terror is not in her book, and so she does not confront Arendt's disquieting contention that "pity, taken as the spring of virtue, has proved to possess a greater capacity for cruelty than cruelty itself."[14] (It is not for nothing that Communist parties, particularly the French one, have always seen 1917 as the logical successor of 1789.)

If humanitarianism could have ambiguous consequences, so could rights themselves. Some historians have attached great significance to the fact that the French, even in 1789, did not proclaim the rights of man alone; they declared the rights of "man and citizen," as part of a paean to the general will. From the outset of the French Revolution, there was a conceptual and political dilemma between membership in humanity and membership in a collective. And what if a choice arose between honoring the rights of men and preserving the

---

13. Arendt, *On Revolution*, p. 89.
14. Ibid.

community of citizens? The doyenne of the field, Hunt has for a few years been insisting that the French Revolution needs to be defended as a progressive victory against those skeptics who would reduce the event to its violence and terror. She deserves great credit for doing so, but it is rather disappointing that she fails to address how revolutionary-era rights might be salvaged from their implication in the bloodshed that so swiftly followed upon their announcement.

The abolition of torture, climaxing in the Revolution, also needs to be understood in a larger context of the changing deployment of violence. In her study of the campaign against torture, Hunt echoes Michel Foucault's view in *Discipline and Punish* that modernity forced the state to relinquish its hold on the body; but while Foucault famously argued that this departure involved more insidious forms of control, Hunt defends it as a good thing. Yet both overlook the fact that the violence involved in what Hunt calls the "sacrificial rite" of punishment under the Old Regime—in which the criminal's public torture provided communal expiation—persisted in novel and magnified forms.[15] As historian David Bell spells out in a fascinating book, the invention of total war over the revolutionary years, whose explosion swamped the world with more devastating violence than ever, was the new and often more frightening guise that public sacrifice could take.[16]

In her last pages, Hunt allows that the rise of humanitarianism and the upsurge of carnage are historical twins, thanks especially to the quintessentially modern penchant

---

15. Hunt, *Inventing Human Rights*, p. 94. This paragraph connects to Paul W. Kahn, *Sacred Violence: Torture, Terror, and Sovereignty* (Ann Arbor, 2008), Chapter 1.

16. David A. Bell, *The First Total War: Napoleon's Europe and the Birth of Warfare as We Know It* (New York, 2007).

to sacrifice oneself and others in war waged for humanity's sake or at least in humanity's name. But she seems not to grasp that this admission amounts to a considerable qualification of her thesis, and she follows this insight with the bland reassurance that empathy "has become a more powerful force for good than ever before."[17]

In contrast to Judt —not to mention Karl Marx, to whose critique of the language of rights she devotes only a desultory page—Hunt is not sensitive to the way that formalistic invocations of rights can sometimes mask narrow agendas. For her, the true significance of this same "abstract universalism" is that it can permit proliferating rights claims. But what is at stake in interpreting the unintended consequences of abstraction is nowhere more in evidence than in recent shifts of views about the meaning of the Haitian uprising of 1791–1803. Until recently, the standard interpretation of the "Black Jacobins" of the Caribbean—in the phrase C. L. R. James gave to his 1938 masterpiece on the subject—saw them as presaging an era of revolutionary nationalism, decolonization and even Third World socialism. Today, in the work of Laurent Dubois and now in Hunt's book, Caribbean antislavery insurgencies are seen as human rights causes. But this idea seems as much a reflection of contemporary passions as the old filiation it displaces.[18]

It is true, as Hunt insists, that Toussaint L'Ouverture and others were spurred by the French Revolution to seize citizenship when the metropolitan government did not live up to its rhetoric. But as the "cascade" did not happen by itself, it had to be forced through violence, and what these radicals insisted on was mainly their right to

---

17. Hunt, *Inventing Human Rights*, p. 212.
18. C. L. R. James, *The Black Jacobins: Toussaint L'Ouverture and the San Domingo Revolution*, revised edition (New York, 1963).

be masters of their fate. Hunt pays homage to "the soft power of humanity." Toussaint, for his part, found it necessary to resort to steely weapons. In any case, the new image of Caribbean insurrection makes one wonder why twentieth-century anticolonialism, the movement from which James took his inspiration, most often eschewed the language of human rights, even though the Universal Declaration had only just been propounded.[19]

The Haitian case suggests another reason the connection between the revolutionary "cascade" and contemporary rights needs to be questioned. For slowly over time, but decisively by the post–World War II era, rights became separated from the revolutionary ambience in which they were originally articulated. As Arendt emphasized, rights in the late eighteenth century were part of revolutionary foundings. But it was nationalism, and even more so socialism, that inherited their radicalism, as well as their tolerance of violence. This is what makes it so difficult to assert any real link between the French Revolution and "human rights" of today. The immediate aftermath of World War II, when the Universal Declaration appeared, partook more of the spirit of restoration than it did of revolution (and the fundamental role of Catholics in the postwar promotion of talk of human rights extended this spirit).

Thus, when Eastern European dissidents made it possible for "human rights" to be reclaimed by liberals and the anti-Communist left in the 1970s, they asserted that what mattered most about those rights is that they were antirevolutionary. Václav Havel and Adam Michnik retrieved human rights precisely

---

19. For further thoughts on Haiti and rights, see my "On the Non-Globalization of Ideas," in Samuel Moyn and Andrew Sartori, eds, *Global Intellectual History* (New York, 2013).

against the tradition of revolution—as an "antipolitics," in Hungarian dissident George Konrád's influential phrase.[20] So human rights arose on the ruins of revolution, not as its descendant. That these figures later played a role in "velvet revolutions" of liberal democracy only reinforces this point. And their fervent support of Bush's war, precisely as a human rights cause, raises new doubts about the defense of rights as an extra-political moral code—the stance that made them famous—and not just about their recent peregrinations.

But the most glaring difficulty in placing the French Revolution at the origins of human rights today is that—unlike dissidence—it gave rise to nothing like the international human rights movement so central to the contemporary moral imagination. It is worth pondering in what ways the campaign to abolish slavery, which began in the years Hunt covers, anticipated contemporary human rights movements. But to do so one would have to move beyond her way of defining human rights so as to see in them a set of institutional practices, prominently including international mobilization, information gathering, public shaming and so forth. Otherwise, there simply was no "rights of man movement" in the nineteenth century—or if there was, it was liberal nationalism, which sought to secure the rights of citizens resolutely in the national framework.

Hunt's position is that nationalism sank the rights of man after their announcement, but from the first they were seen as overlapping or even identical commitments. (The Declaration of the Rights of Man and Citizen insists that "no body and no individual may exercise authority which does not emanate expressly from the

---

20. George Konrád, *Antipolitics* (New York, 1984).

nation.")[21] True, there were occasional proto-interna-
tionalist moments in the era, as for example in the
presence in the National Assembly of the amusingly
named Anacharsis Cloots, a German baron who considered himself the voice of non-French humanity. (Among
other things, he begged for military action against his
own people.) But such innovations hardly pointed ahead
to the United Nations or anticipated the contemporary
realities of international law and international groups
sprouting in civil society to pressure governments to
obey it. (Cloots surfaces in Herman Melville's *Moby-
Dick*, in fact, as the symbol of multicultural humanity
united on shipboard in a metaphysical quest, not for
prophesying an international legal regime.[22])

If rights had any internationalist pedigree flowing from
the French Revolution, it was, alas, mainly to be found in
Napoleon Bonaparte's claim to be spreading the flame of
the rights of man as he engulfed the world in the confla-
gration of his imperial designs. "Oh ye Egyptians,"
Napoleon proclaimed in 1798 in advertising his conquest
as a benevolent act, "they may say to you that I have not
made an expedition hither for any other object than that
of abolishing your religion . . . But tell the slanderers that
I have not come to you except for the purpose of restor-
ing your rights from the hands of the oppressors."[23]

21. For further thoughts, see my "Giuseppe Mazzini in (and Beyond)
the History of Human Rights," in Miia Halme-Tuomisaari and Pamela
Slotte, eds, *Human Rights and Other Histories* (forthcoming).

22. Herman Melville, *Moby-Dick; or, The Whale* (New York, 2001),
p. 132. See Hallman B. Bryant, "The Anarcharsis Cloots Deputation,"
American Notes and Queries 19, nos 7–8 (March 1981): 107–9, noting
that Melville alludes to Cloots in a similar spirit in two other novels,
likely relying on Thomas Carlyle's depiction of the German baron in
The French Revolution.

23. Cited in Daniel W. Brown, *A New Introduction to Islam* (New
York, 2011), p. 251.

Omitting the longstanding imperial entanglements of both humanitarianism and rights simply will not do; history shows how frequently they have been offered as justifications for invasion, expansion and annexation. This is not to say that the revolutionary rights of man anticipated George W. Bush and neoconservative empire, rather than a universalistic regime of international law; merely that one cannot embrace rights in the distant past without acknowledging their radically different futures.

Each of these diverse perspectives on revolutionary-era rights forces the same recognition. In order for the contemporary human rights movement to emerge, old meanings and associations had to be dropped and new ones formed. What Hunt presents as an epilogue to a creation long ago turns out to be what really needs explaining. This is what Marc Bloch meant when, in *The Historian's Craft*, he indicted "the idol of origins." A distant precondition for something is never its cause or trigger, and even continuity in history has to be explained in virtue of not just the long run but also the short term.

When, then, were human rights invented? As Hunt admits, the phrase hardly ever shows up in English in her period. And while it percolated in diplomatic and legal circles beginning in the 1940s, it was not until the 1970s, with the emergence of dissident movements in Eastern Europe, that it entered common parlance. This is the period that historians need to scrutinize most intently—the moment when human rights triumphed as a set of beliefs and as the stimulus for new activities and institutions, particularly non-governmental organizations. Yet the minds of human rights scholars constantly wander backward—disinclined, it seems, to face up to the recent vintage and contingent beginnings of their subject.

Of course, with the founding of the United Nations and its Universal Declaration (along with related instruments like the genocide convention, as well as the beginnings of intra-European rights protection), the 1940s were of obvious significance. But if there is little reason to locate the "invention" of human rights as we now know them in the late eighteenth century, there are scarcely more grounds for rooting them in World War II's aftermath.

Currently, a powerful movement among American historians portrays contemporary human rights as flowing directly and fully formed out of Franklin Delano Roosevelt's wartime vision and planning, much as Athena sprang from Zeus's skull. For this school, the internationalist rights agenda is an American invention that extended and supplemented the nation's original commitment to liberty with more full-bodied social protection. In Elizabeth Borgwardt's phrase, human rights were America's "new deal for the world."[24] The wistfully nostalgic tones of the historians of an invigorating and well-intentioned American liberalism are poignant and can lead to insight. But there are serious objections—political and interpretive—to this story.

For one thing, it makes human rights seem like the natural outcome of the last consensual war, an uncontroversial good that emerged in response to incontestable evil (never mind that the assertion of rights bore little relationship to the Nazi genocide). Second, it Americanizes rights, evoking a time when the US government could be seen as a benevolent guarantor of universal norms of conduct. Self-evidently, the actual

---

24. Elizabeth Borgwardt, *A New Deal for the World: America's Vision for Human Rights* (Cambridge, MA, 2006).

content of the portrayal of human rights as the product of a moment when America offered a genuine universalism is the contemporary moral it allows: that Bush's worst sin is to have ruined the storyline that began with America's invention of human rights in the 1940s and was finally on the way to fruition thanks to Bill Clinton's commitment to enforce them in the 1990s.

As David Rieff has argued, affirming America's universalistic self-image in the past (as the city on a hill, the leader of the free world, or the indispensable nation) is to fail to ask just how it was that Bush was able to succeed so easily in burnishing the morality of his adventures—as if what went wrong were a purely accidental perversion of America's true and proper vocation.[25] But there are also historical distortions. Scholars who return to the 1940s, like Borgwardt and Cass Sunstein, devote little or no attention to non-American contributions to "rights talk" in the era, and exaggerate its importance and impact at the time.[26] They select and single out what now look like milestones, because of their retroactive importance, but fail to grasp their marginality in their own period, from which no broad-gauged international movement emerged. Once again, historians are choosing tunnel vision over historical sense.

None of this means that the new fashion of human rights history is entirely misguided. Only those who missed the last thirty years of ideological history—like certain Marxists who regard "human rights" as nothing but a rhetoric that makes the cage of globalizing neoliberalism more bearable—could think so.[27] But it does mean that

25. David Rieff, "We Are the World," the *Nation*, June 14, 2006.

26. Cass R. Sunstein, *The Second Bill of Rights: FDR's Unfinished Revolution and Why We Need It More Than Ever* (New York, 2004).

27. Slavoj Žižek, "Against Human Rights," *New Left Review*, n.s., 34 (July-August 2005): 115–31.

we need to understand that human rights in their specific contemporary connotations are an invention of recent date, which drew on prior languages and practices the way a chemical reaction depends on having various elements around from different sources, some of them older than others. The explosion took place only yesterday, and we have to come to grips with why it happened and what the costs and benefits have been for us all. The fact that it only recently occurred to historians to uncover the origins of human rights is itself a sign that they should not seek to find them too long ago and far away.

But there is also a strategic consideration. Human rights norms and organizations remain the chief source of idealistic passion in the world—at least among its well-meaning cosmopolitan elites. Any future idealism will have to draw on the power of their current ethic and put it to good use. In this regard, Hunt is exactly right to stress the emotional charge of human rights. But besides lacking any coherent understanding of how human rights came to have their current power, we have not even begun thinking about how to reinvent the creed in ways that are progressive rather than brutal.

In closing what feels in the end like a creation myth, Hunt writes: "The human rights framework, with its international bodies, international courts, and international conventions, might be exasperating in its slowness to respond or repeated inability to achieve its ultimate goals, but there is no better structure available for confronting these issues."[28] For better or worse, the plangent reassurances have lost their power to comfort, and deep background—especially when brought to bear so instrumentally on our very different present—is of little use in allaying our confusion and dismay.

---

28. Hunt, *Inventing Human Rights*, p. 213.

2

THE SURPRISING ORIGINS
OF HUMAN DIGNITY

"A king's head is solemnly oiled at his coronation, even as a head of salad," Ishmael jokes in Herman Melville's *Moby-Dick*, in the course of cataloging every last use of whale blubber. "Much might be ruminated here, concerning the essential dignity of this regal process," he adds. "Dignity" appears twenty times in Melville's novel, and usually refers to the high standing of offices and activities—including, inevitably, whaling. But most often, dignity pertains to monarchs, and the humorous treatment that somehow elevates kings does not work its magic on everyone. For Ishmael, the notion that democracy offers everyone the dignified prerogatives of kings seems mistaken, if not ridiculous. "In truth, a mature man who uses hair-oil," he surmises, "can't amount to much in his totality."[1]

In *Dignity, Rank, and Rights*, Jeremy Waldron, perhaps the leading legal and political philosopher of our day, argues that the notion of human dignity originated in the democratization of the high social status

---

1. Herman Melville, *Moby-Dick; or, The Whale* (New York, 2001), p. 123.

once reserved for the well-born.[2] "Dignity" means rank, and Waldron argues that we are the beneficiaries of a long, gradual process he calls "leveling up." More and more people, he says, are treated as high-status individuals, deserving of the social respect once restricted to the solemnly oiled. In an age of human rights, everyone can become a king, at least on paper or in court, where claims that basic human dignity is non-negotiable have achieved a remarkable presence in the last few years.

Since the end of World War II, nobody besides conservative and typically Catholic thinkers had staked philosophical systems on the notion of human dignity, but liberal philosophers like Waldron are flocking to it to revitalize theories of political ethics. Around the same time as Waldron turned to dignity, the late Ronald Dworkin, in his masterwork *Justice for Hedgehogs* (2011), claimed that it is the most basic value society should advance. Jürgen Habermas, the great German thinker, recently admitted that human dignity had not featured as the cited authority for human rights for most of modern history, whether in 1776 in Virginia or 1789 in France or thereafter; he concluded from this fact that dignity must have been implicit to human rights all along. That cannot be correct. During most of that time dignity served to elevate some people over others, rather than putting them on the same level.[3] And when dignity did finally enter politics—mysteriously encoded at mid-century in the United Nations Charter, the Universal Declaration of Human Rights (1948), and West German

---

2. Jeremy Waldron, *Dignity, Rank, and Rights*, ed. Meir Dan-Cohen (New York, 2012).

3. Ronald Dworkin, *Justice for Hedgehogs* (Cambridge, MA, 2011); Jürgen Habermas, "The Concept of Human Dignity and the Realistic Utopia of Human Rights," in *The Crisis of the European Union: A Response*, translated by Ciaran Cronin (Malden, 2012).

constitutional Basic Law (1949)—it was not the watchword in philosophy or political theory that it has
become. Which leads to a question: what is in the
water—other than fewer whales than in Melville's day?

Before the modern era, dignity was not considered to
be an inviolable value. The Renaissance guru Pico della
Mirandola, who wrote an oration in the fifteenth
century later called "On the Dignity of Man," is often
regarded as a confused precursor of later understandings of it. (In *Dignity: Its History and Meaning*,
Harvard political theorist Michael Rosen treats Pico
this way.[4]) But Pico, a Cabbalist and magician, was too
idiosyncratic a thinker to be anyone's ancestor.[5] After
all, he insisted that what makes humans different than
everything else in the universe is their lack of any
defined essence. As contemporary Italian philosopher
Giorgio Agamben has noted, Pico's discourse "does
not contain the term *dignitas*, which . . . could not in
any case refer to man. For the central thesis of the
oration is that man, having been molded when the
models of creation were all used up, can have neither
archetype nor proper place nor specific rank."[6]

In modern times, Alexis de Tocqueville was the first
to write about the democratization of high standing. A
French aristocrat who travelled to America to size up a
newfangled thing called "democracy," Tocqueville
warned that if aristocratic values were not somehow

---

4. Michael Rosen, *Dignity: Its History and Meaning* (Cambridge,
MA, 2012).

5. See especially Brian P. Copenhaver, "Magic and the Dignity of
Man: De-Kanting Pico's *Oration*," in A. J. Grieco et al., eds., *The
Italian Renaissance in the Twentieth Century* (Florence, 2002).

6. Giorgio Agamben, *The Open: Man and Animal*, translated by
Kevin Attell (Stanford, 2004), p. 29.

preserved after the departure of feudal kings and nobles, humanity would be debased. "In aristocratic ages vast ideas are commonly entertained of the dignity, the power, and the greatness of man," he noted.[7] Democracy might promise leveling up but mainly threatened to flatten distinctions altogether—a risk which neither Waldron nor other current chroniclers of dignity seem to take seriously. But even on its own terms, there are problems with Waldron's argument.

Aristocratic social status is not an innate characteristic: ask the riff-raff who have bought or married into it over the centuries. And even for those who lucked into high birth, their standing was always ritually established, as the ceremonial anointing of kings suggests. For nobles, social requirements included dress, language, manners and manor, and for males also involved the sort of repetitious violence and denigration of the body that we now think human dignity is supposed to deter or forbid. Nineteenth-century aristocrats, in their last gasp of importance, whiled away their idle hours rattling sabers, and when not preparing to fight were engaged in nasty duels, giving one another the physical scars that were frequently the mandatory signs of their superiority.[8] Such rituals, like anointing, seem fairly silly when applied to everyone; besides, discussions about human dignity consider it to be "inherent." It is not something that elaborate social

---

7. Alexis de Tocqueville, *Democracy in America*, translated by George Lawrence (New York, 1966), p. 462. James Whitman revived Tocqueville before Waldron further theorized dignity as rank. See, for instance, James Q. Whitman, "Enforcing Civility and Respect: Three Societies," *Yale Law Journal* 109 (2000): 1279–1398.

8. See Peter Gay, "*Mensur*: The Cherished Scar," in *The Cultivation of Hatred* (New York, 1993), which emphasizes the bourgeois expansion of bodily invasion in nineteenth-century German lands.

rituals, and least of all bodily violence, are required to establish.

The historical origins of dignity in social status are important to Waldron because of the recent popularity of the turn to another potential source—abstract philosophy—for securing human worth. Even as dignity was slowly being recognized as existing beyond aristocrats, philosophers continued their age-old struggle to identify some uniquely human properties that set us above the other animals. One philosopher, however, the sage of the German Enlightenment Immanuel Kant, thought about human distinction precisely in terms of dignity— namely, the priceless worth conferred on us by our freedom to choose.[9] Kant inserted a break in the great chain of being between the rest of the animals, which are purely subject to the determination of nature's laws, and human beings, who could (he hoped) deploy their free will to make their own rules rather than slavishly obey beastly imperatives. In a difficult argument, Kant insisted that man's "rational nature," our ability to set ends, makes everyone of highest value, and indeed provides the basis of all value in the world. His metaphysical promotion of the centrality of human dignity is significant intellectually because, as Rosen remarks, it is on Kant's "giant shoulders the modern theory of human rights rests" nowadays.[10]

Waldron, whose latest book is typically careful, lucid, and subtle, seems openly nervous about resting everything on those shoulders. In practical terms, he suggests that it is best to establish people's worth in the future not by abstract and controversial claims like Kant's

---

9. See, e.g., Thomas E. Hill, Jr., *Dignity and Practical Reason in Kant's Moral Theory* (Ithaca, 1992). I believe it was the first book ever written in English emphasizing dignity in Kant's thought.

10. Rosen, *Dignity*, p. 19.

about their freedom and autonomy, which do not command universal agreement, but rather by letting the law work slowly to grant them higher status, as has been the case in constitutional and international human rights law during the last few decades. Further, as Waldron persuasively argues, it's not possible to derive from Kant's idea of human dignity all that human rights law might protect. For example, the Universal Declaration makes room for economic and social protections, but how can the notion of human dignity justify the declaration's more specific protection of unionization rights or paid vacations?

The partisans of a metaphysical basis for human dignity might respond, predictably, that what goes up can go down. And ultimately some knockdown argument is required to establish the grounds for treating human beings as inherently precious. Social status is a powerful source of norms, but it is no necessary basis for improving treatment. The arc of the moral universe is definitely long, as our president likes to say, but it does not bend towards justice unless pushed. Waldron's proposal is that the universal and egalitarian implications of Kant's kingdom of ends can be reached indirectly by allowing the democratization of high status to continue through various legal institutions. But it is hard to see why anyone could be confident about this bet—unless Waldron were, like Tocqueville (or Barack Obama), committed to the view that history inevitably betters humanity's lot. But at this late date it is naïve to appeal to the workings of providence. In fact, a closer look at the historical details of dignity's trajectory suggests that its prominence today is directly related to a crisis of progress.

There is a big omission in the view that dignity is the rank due to high social status: the lord at the top of the totem pole, God. In *Moby-Dick*, Ishmael allows that dignity still exists in the natural kingdom, where divine majesty remains intact even if America has shown the world that men can rule themselves. "In the great Sperm Whale, this high and mighty god-like dignity inherent in the brow is so immensely amplified," he remarks, "that gazing on it, in that full front view, you feel the Deity and the dread powers more forcibly than in beholding any other object in living nature."[11] This is the sort of dignity that matters to Captain Ahab, famously obsessed with the Deity who refuses to answer him—and for whom the white whale stands in as proxy.

Unlike Ishmael, Ahab fears the loss of dignity resulting from the departure or silence of God. He fears that when belief in a God on high wanes, humanity's worth and purpose is thrown radically into doubt. As the literary critic Robert Milder argues in his magnificent study of Melville, *Exiled Royalties*, "Ahab craves recognition that he is heaven-born and, if not heaven-destined, then at least, by nature and bearing, heaven-worthy . . . If God will not condescend to him by word or sign, Ahab will extort the sign, if only by forcing God to kill him."[12] By extension, *Moby-Dick* explores how human dignity ultimately depends on (and comes from) a theological principle, not a political or social one alone.

Kings and aristocrats relied heavily on a theological worldview, with God establishing their "divine right" for the rule of his noble representatives on earth. In fact, it is extremely doubtful that Kant's bundle of assumptions about what makes human beings dignified can be plausibly traced to European beliefs about social status,

---

11. Melville, *Moby-Dick*, p. 379.

12. Robert Milder, *Exiled Royalties: Melville and the Life We Imagine* (Oxford, 2006), p. 98.

as opposed to theological premises which he struggled to reformulate in secular terms. As the nineteenth century passed, and Kant's thought fell out of favor (Arthur Schopenhauer called dignity "the shibboleth of all empty-headed moralists"), the party most closely associated with claims about human dignity was neither liberal nor socialist but conservative and rigid in its commitment to hierarchy: the Catholic Church.

In his penetrating and sprightly essay on human dignity, Rosen rightly emphasizes the centrality of Catholicism to the modern history of claims on human dignity. His command of the history is impressive, but his chiefly philosophical purpose leads him to overlook some dramatic historical developments or note them only in passing. Rosen leaves the impression that human dignity rose as a kind of common ground between liberal Kantians and post-Holocaust Catholics, who agreed that our humanity is the source of moral worth, but differed slightly about its implications. But no Kantians were around when it mattered: at mid-century, when the UN Charter, Universal Declaration and German Constitution were written. Furthermore, Rosen throws up his hands when it comes to explaining how political Catholicism, mostly closely associated with human dignity in the 1930s, was changed by fascism and war, which in turn proved crucial to the re-invocation of dignity in the 1940s.

Rosen beautifully shows, however, that Catholic dignity long bolstered the vision of a highly hierarchical society. In the confusing decade of the 1930s, when Catholic social thought profoundly informed the illiberal regimes in Austria, Portugal, and Spain, dignity seemed to refer to man's place in a divine order in which the high "rank" of humans still meant their subordination to one another—and notably the subordination of women to men. The first constitution to feature human dignity in a prominent way dates from Ireland in 1937, where "the freedom and dignity of the individual" is linked to theological virtues, and women were told—contrary to the country's earlier liberal constitution which the new document repealed—to find their "place in the home."[13] And the notion of human dignity invoked by the Church forbade the egalitarian solutions of communism—which promised to "level up" humanity more than liberals have. But Catholics in the 1930s were not yet sure whether the protection of dignity was served by liberal democracy, or threatened by it almost as frighteningly as by communism itself.

Some Catholic dissidents, however, argued against the alliance of Catholicism and reaction, advocating instead for a moralistic conservatism compatible with, or even dependent on, a liberal democracy whose viability had long been doubted in mainstream Catholic circles. When the Allied victory in World War II swept the table of reactionary politics (except in Iberia), Catholics began to link human dignity with parliamentary democracy and "human rights." But even then, Catholics wanted to separate human dignity from the potentially anarchistic implications of individual human rights. "The holy story of Christmas proclaims this inviolable dignity of man with a vigor and authority that cannot be gainsaid," Pope Pius XII observed in a hugely influential message in late 1944, "an authority and vigor that infinitely transcends that which all possible declarations of the rights

---

13. I explore these matters in my "The Secret History of Constitutional Dignity," in Christopher McCrudden, ed., *Understanding Human Dignity* (Oxford, 2013), and in a longer version in *Yale Human Rights and Development Law Journal*, forthcoming.

of man could achieve." Human rights having long been associated with the French Revolution's legacy, no wonder the pope was nervous about them. And so the most unfortunate fact in the history of human dignity is that, when the notion entered world politics in Christian hands, it had been severed from a revolutionary legacy thought at the time to be a slippery slope to communism and a road to serfdom.

The political theorist Charles Beitz has recently discovered that it was Barnard College dean Virginia Gildersleeve who altered the preamble of the UN Charter in San Francisco in 1945 to include its current reference to "the dignity and worth of the human person." The language seems most traceable to Catholic usage, because no one else invoked the idea during wartime. One thing is clear: the appearance of human dignity in the charter was surely not an evocation of a principle violated by the European Holocaust, because the Jews were of no serious concern to either Pius XII or Gildersleeve. The latter had spent much of the 1930s trying to bar Jews from her school, and she gave speeches sympathetic to Germany's territorial expansion. After the war, as the historian Stephen Norwood has shown, Gildersleeve's "campaign" against what she called "International Zionism" testified to "the inability of many . . . to comprehend the depth . . . of Jewish suffering."[14] The same is true in postwar West Germany, where the annunciation of dignity suited the agendas of its time.

The main one, it seems, was the rise of Christian Democracy, a conservative political movement that

---

14. Stephen H. Norwood, *The Third Reich in the Ivory Tower: Complicity and Conflict on American Campuses* (Cambridge, 2009), p. 130.

established dominance in Western Europe in which appeals to "human dignity" figured by far most commonly. In the history of postwar constitutions, after Ireland's pioneering usage, dignity appeared first in conservative Catholic Bavaria's constitution in 1946, then in that of Christian Democratic Italy in 1947, before the West German constitution was written with its now famous first article: "Human dignity is inviolable." And indeed, the enduring influence of Catholic premises on West German legal thought shaped dignity's meaning for a long time. Rosen seriously overstates the Kantian influence in the original West German constitution and its early interpretation. The figure he cites as a Kantian interpreter, Günter Dürig, drew his influential interpretation of dignity and other precepts of constitutional law as "objective values" from one of Kant's most incisive modern critics, sometime Catholic philosopher Max Scheler.[15]

After 1945, Westerners generally followed the example of the Catholics in the previous decade and used the notion of dignity to attack communism. A founding document of American Cold War politics, NSC-68, says the point of the campaign is the defense of human dignity, and President Harry Truman agreed that "both religion and democracy are founded on one basic principle, the worth and dignity of the individual man and

---

15. Günter Dürig, "Die Menschenauffassung des Grundgesetzes," *Juristische Rundschau* 7 (1952): 259–63, reprinted in *Gesammelte Schriften*, Walter Schmitt Glaeser and Peter Häberle, eds. (Berlin, 1984). Cf. Ernst-Wolfgang Böckenförde, "Die Menschenwürde *war* unantastbar," *Frankfurter Allgemeine Zeitung*, September 9, 2003. See also Frieder Günther, *Denken vom Staat her: Die bundesdeutsche Staatsrechtslehre zwischen Dezision und Integration 1949–1970* (Munich, 2004), pp. 193–6.

woman."[16] But this Cold War rhetoric as much obstructed its currency as guaranteed its centrality.

With that rhetoric's gradual dissolution, human dignity became open to new interpretations. At least in Western Europe, public Christianity collapsed. There and elsewhere, Kant became popular thanks to the publication in 1971 of John Rawls's *Theory of Justice*, which suddenly established individual rights as the indispensable foundation of social justice. (Interestingly, Rawls himself never focused on dignity, but the retrieval of Kant he inspired eventually got there—though, as Rosen shows in one of his most impressive discussions, it was in a far more secular key than Kant's texts permit.) Finally, and at first independently, a new sort of international human rights movement arose, one initially focused on bodily violations like torture which a global public came to regard as the most egregious violations of dignity.[17] When the Cold War ended, it became possible to surmise that most people, after all, agree about the dictates of "dignity" and other basic values, even though they spent the twentieth century slaughtering one another over which ideals to prize.

Rosen is a wonderful guide to recent German constitutional thinking about dignity crafted in this new climate. Today, he shows, West German dignity is generally secular, liberal and even Kantian in its meaning, notably in a controversial decision made after 9/11 forbidding the state from shooting down an airliner captured by terrorists. (Rosen also has amusing discussions of dwarf-tossing and other current controversies, and is in general an

---

16. William Inboden, *Religion and American Foreign Policy, 1945–1960: The Soul of Containment* (Cambridge, 2008), p. 109 and *passim* for copious evidence of dignity in American Cold War discourse.

17. See below, Chapter 7.

urbane and witty companion, achieving his aim of accessibly written philosophy.) Dignity is a feature of nearly all constitutions written lately, especially South Africa's exemplary and prestigious document. Basic conflicts are easily reframed in terms of dignity: the dignity of life of infants used to be set off against women's liberation in abortion debates, but defenders of choice long ago learned to deploy dignity too.

Yet dignity's religious sources make it hard for secular progressives to claim it easily or unambiguously. The 2012 Democratic Party platform referred to dignity frequently, in association with the universal human rights that liberals in the United States say are the country's foundation, including emphasis on global women's rights and global development, as well in relation to liberal social policy like health care. Yet the Republican platform invoked dignity just as frequently: to inveigh against abortion and explain why it is wrong (one reason being that it offends "the dignity of women"), to insist that marriage is exclusively for heterosexuals, and to support the military, warning that it must not become the site of "social experimentation." In these usages, dignity clearly refers to a moral code above and beyond society, to which democracy must defer.[18]

Not even Ishmael thought dignity could be a purely secular ideal. He is nonchalant by comparison to Captain Ahab—but that's a low bar. Ishmael is an exile too (and the namesake of one), but not, like Ahab, exercised about it. He is even complacent about God's fickle

---

18. Compare the two documents, Democratic National Committee, "Moving America Forward," posted at http://assets.dstatic.org/dnc-platform/2012-National-Platform.pdf, 1, 2, 28, 29, 30, and Republican National Committee, "We Believe in America," posted at http://www.gop.com/wp-content/uploads/2012/08/2012GOPplatform.pdf, 13, 31, 33, 42, 44.

disappearance, however much he allows himself to be temporarily seduced by Ahab's quest. He has no place in the world, and usually does not seem concerned about his metaphysical standing.[19] Yet strangely, when he celebrates democracy, Ishmael does so precisely in terms of the godly dignity that he mocked earlier, when describing kings and their coronations. "Men may seem detestable as joint stock-companies and nations; knaves, fools, and murderers there may be; men may have mean and meagre faces," Ishmael muses,

> but man, in the ideal, is so noble and so sparkling, such a grand and glowing creature, that over any ignominious blemish in him all his fellows should run to throw their costliest robes . . . [T]his august dignity I treat of, is not the dignity of kings and robes, but that abounding dignity which has no robed investiture. [It is] that democratic dignity which, on all hands, radiates without end from God; Himself! The great God absolute! The centre and circumference of all democracy! His omnipresence, our divine equality![20]

Ishmael's "faith" is rousing. But how can Melville's character salvage anointed worth from the overthrown order in which kings and aristocrats acted as the dignified intermediaries between God and everyone else? And if men need robes to hide their blemishes, how can they do without "robed investiture" of some kind? Most important, how could Ishmael appeal so effortlessly to God, and the human dignity based on Him, as if it were not the very premise that Ahab needed to test in his fiery hunt?

Searching for divine certification of our standing may

---

19. Milder, *Exiled Royalties*, pp. 89–91.
20. Melville, *Moby-Dick*, p. 126.

always be appealing, but the liberal interest in dignity seems to follow from less exalted and metaphysical concerns. When the French Revolution and the struggle for the freedoms of blacks, women, and workers were being won across the nineteenth century, no theories of human dignity were required. Human rights in particular were unconnected to dignity, outside Kant, until Catholics yoked them together at mid-century. Today human dignity is a principle chiefly for those who admire judges and want them to have the power to check the state in the name of basic humanitarian values.[21] Its currency is a sign that our morality has been redefined around the worst that can transpire in history, rather than some better order that could be achieved through political contest and struggle. A consensus about dignity may have become deep enough for us to insist the state not torture, but it has proved far less helpful when some of us insist that our fellow humans care about one another's broader welfare or collective emancipation. Isn't that undignified?

21. Erin Daly, *Dignity Rights: Courts, Constitutions, and the Worth of the Human Person* (Philadelphia, 2012).

3

SPECTACULAR WRONGS: ON
HUMANITARIAN INTERVENTION

The most troubling fact about international politics in
the nineteenth century is not that moral appeals to save
suffering humanity were absent, but that they were
everywhere. The British, who led the international
campaign to end the slave trade, and then slavery,
abused that credential by tirelessly citing their national
moral superiority as a justification for imperial rule—
including invasion and expansion. The crimes of savage
peoples and backward states had to be stopped, and the
British—self-styled agents of humane values—were the
ones to do it. "Nations which are still barbarous," even
liberal John Stuart Mill explained, "have not got beyond
the period during which it is likely to be for their benefit
that they should be conquered and held in subjection by
foreigners."[1] Among many other expressions of enlightened humanitarianism, such rhetoric justified numerous
"small wars" in the hinterlands, where the civilizing
constraints on armed conflict that Europeans had

---

1. John Stuart Mill, "A Few Words about Non-Intervention," in
Gertrude Himmelfarb, ed., *The Spirit of the Age: Victorian Essays*
(New Haven, 2007), p. 166.

developed for their contests were neither suspended nor disobeyed because they did not apply in the first place. As Lytton Strachey might have put it, the history of Victorian humanitarianism will never be written: we know too much about it.

Gary Bass thinks otherwise. In *Freedom's Battle*, he claims that the European nineteenth century is a precious and neglected resource for anyone who wants to champion human rights in contemporary politics, especially when atrocities take place in distant lands, provided that the suffering is accurately depicted by a free and disinterested press and armed intervention is the only alternative to standing idly by while evildoers slaughter the innocent.[2] Bass recovers a few early cases of humanitarian intervention he considers legitimate in order to supply today's humanitarians with a noble tradition that can be invoked against conservative realists, leftist anti-imperialists, and academic nitpickers who doubt the virtues of "humanitarian intervention."

To his credit, Bass is aware of the long and sordid history in the West, going back to the European discovery of the New World and intensifying in the nineteenth century, of false claims to care about foreign evil and human suffering—and co-optations of true claims to false ends. Surveying the decidedly mixed history of intervention a century ago in the first English-language treatise on the subject, Ellery Stowell admitted that only a few invocations of humanity passed the straight-face test, since they typically featured high-minded rhetoric

---

2. Gary J. Bass, *Freedom's Battle: The Origins of Humanitarian Intervention* (New York, 2008). For more recent histories of humanitarian intervention, see Brendan Simms and D. J. B. Trim, eds, *Humanitarian Intervention: A History* (Cambridge, 2011) and Davide Rodogno, *Against Massacre: Humanitarian Interventions in the Ottoman Empire, 1815–1914* (Princeton, 2011).

masking low-minded imperialism. "In this polite age," he wrote, "conquest is usually effected [through] war proclaimed to have been undertaken in defense of international law rights."[3] The most notorious humanitarian imperialist of the polite age was probably King Leopold of Belgium, who took the gift of the Congo from the great powers, promising to eliminate vile slavery and bring civilization, then turned the country into his private extraction ranch and a nest of untold cruelty. Bass knows that Victorian humanitarianism often exported to foreign lands the savagery it purported to be banishing from them. He simply asks the reader to bracket such contradictions at the outset and see if anything noble is left to be salvaged; he wants us to acknowledge the generally tainted nature of nineteenth-century humanitarianism and move on. "There were some important episodes even in a horribly imperialistic age," he writes. "There were, and are, real universalists."[4]

The cornerstones of Bass's argument are accounts of British outrage about Ottoman repression in Greece in the 1820s and in Bulgaria in the 1870s. Bass's main protagonists are Lord Byron and William Gladstone, cast as a selfless activist and a selfless politician, respectively. Byron agitated for Greek freedom fighters under the Muslim yoke, which became especially oppressive in a bloodbath on the island of Chios. Besides exciting an enthusiastic international fan club by relaying the Greek cries for help ("For foreign arms and aid they fondly sigh," he wrote in *Childe Harold's Pilgrimage*), Byron traveled to war and died a Romantic hero's death.[5]

---

3. Ellery C. Stowell, *Intervention in International Law* (Washington, DC, 1921), p. 436.

4. Bass, *Freedom's Battle*, pp. 6, 351.

5. *The Complete Poetical and Dramatic Works of Lord Byron* (Philadelphia, 1883), p. 20.

Fifty years later, and out of office after a lost election, Gladstone staged what turned into a political comeback by drafting a heated denunciation of the savage Ottoman repression of Bulgarian nationalists and then pressuring Britain's conservative government to stop it, ultimately riding popular emotion all the way to a second term as prime minister. In both cases, intervention eventually led to local independence, at least for a while. Bass complements these British set pieces with accounts of the French expedition to Syria in the 1860s to save Christians from local depredations and Ottoman misrule, and international concern about the oppression of Armenians, once again at Ottoman hands, during the lead-up to World War I, when it became genocide.

Bass's accounts of these events are well-crafted, tacked down by vivid turns of phrase plucked from the prose of eminent Victorians. One of the most revealing of his rhetorical devices is to make the Ottoman massacres sound a lot like the Holocaust, though the former were, in the nineteenth century, more "ordinary" counterinsurgencies against territorially based bids for secession—themselves violent in their methods—in which the West took sides. Bass amusingly names the repression of the Greeks "A Problem from Hellas," a riff on the title of Samantha Power's well-known book about genocide, and he makes sure to convey that people at the time thought "immediate and total annihilation" was occurring as part of a grim plan "to extirpate systematically a whole community." He even finds Gladstone proclaiming, "Never again."[6]

The "atrocitarian" cause may touch our hearts, but

6. Bass, *Freedom's Battle*, pp. 55, 69, 127, 277, alluding to Samantha Power, *"A Problem from Hell": America and the Age of Genocide* (New York, 2003).

can cherry-picked cases really win over our minds about nineteenth-century do-goodery? It's a question worth asking, since Bass, after admitting he has bracketed much evidence that contradicts his heroic presentation of these episodes, goes on to champion them anyway. And whatever evidence of impure motives or mixed causes he does introduce, he excuses. Of course the Victorians were arrogant, Bass readily admits, and given their imperial consciousness, it may be that they wanted to soften their hegemony with some humanitarianism. But establishing hegemony through political influence, culture and markets is different from running an empire, he explains, and once in a while Europeans forswore formal rule. The most remarkable feature of *Freedom's Battle* is that its author is constantly apologizing for the very heroes he claims he can surgically extract from the compromising circumstances of their times. In a pamphlet denouncing the Bulgarian atrocities, Gladstone offered a farrago of Christianity and racism, Bass records. These facts make Gladstone's words "an unlikely kind of Magna Carta for the human rights movement," he concedes, but he treats it as one all the same, as if writing history were about skimming the dross off the parts you like.

Some vital roots of humanitarianism are left unexcavated in *Freedom's Battle*, and they reach back to the Protestant revolution of sentiment in the sixteenth and seventeenth centuries. The revolution began when Protestant divines started to emphasize the importance of good works and the feelings of pity on which they were based. The idea was that while the project of reforming the world in a Christian spirit could not directly compel God to elect you, it would prepare Christian communities for salvation and demonstrate to

God their eligibility for it. The key ingredient of this revolution was sympathy, the capacity to identify with the suffering of others, which enabled charitable practices to be built on an interior emotional and spiritual foundation.[7]

In eighteenth-century Britain, this revolution sparked an explosion of compassion in intellectual circles and popular culture. Partly secularized in the so-called sentimentalist philosophy of David Hume and Adam Smith and in the sentimental novels of Samuel Richardson and Laurence Sterne, the new emotional code became an established fixture among European and even American elites by the turn of the nineteenth century. "Nature hath implanted in our breasts a love of others, a sense of duty to them, a moral instinct, in short, which prompts us irresistibly to feel and to succor their distresses," Thomas Jefferson wrote in a letter to Thomas Law in 1814.[8] Bill Clinton was not the first president of the United States to feel your pain.

Bass associates such modern fellow-feeling with liberal solidarity, but the proposition is dubious, unless liberalism is defined in a historically careful way. In the eighteenth and nineteenth centuries, sympathy was usually a manifestation not of egalitarian solidarity with downtrodden strangers but of *noblesse oblige*. As the literary historian Lynn Festa has shown, humanitarianism established in the imagination powerful hierarchical relationships between the compassionate and the suffering, and worked in tandem with imperial and market

---

7. On religious sources, see my "Empathy in History, Empathizing with Humanity," *History and Theory* 45, no. 3 (October 2006): 397–415.

8. Merrill D. Peterson, ed., *The Political Writings of Thomas Jefferson* (Raleigh, 1993), p. 176.

expansion.[9] There is more than a trace of these origins in
Bass's suggestion that atrocities basically happen elsewhere, and in distant lands, with the result that great
powers (which is to say, advanced countries) will never
lose their assigned role of guarding against the ever
threatening scandal of barbarity. "Massacres turn out
to be the regular way of the world," Bass writes.
Bloodbaths occurred in "remote places like Greece and
Bulgaria" a century ago, and they crop up in "some far-
off corner of the globe" today.[10] Then and now, the
message is: Stop the Violence—Over There.

As it became a political ethos, guiding a vast array of
private activities as well as state action (sometimes military), sentimental humanitarianism fell prey to four
interlocking syndromes. First, sentimentalism promoted
a culture of sensationalism. "The roots of British inter-
ventionism lay in Printing-House Square," Bass says.
True, but so did the roots of a lot of other things. As
activists churned out stories and pictures of suffering for
their middle-class publics, they invited the charge that
their daily accounts of outrage abroad merely excited
readers instead of goading them to action. Sometimes
the inundation of the public sphere with narratives and
pictures of corporal violence had quite counterintuitive
results: one of the first diagnosed sadists in history was
a man who found the humanitarian depiction of tortured
slaves in *Uncle Tom's Cabin* sexually exciting.[11]

Accentuating the positive, Bass contends that there is
a lawlike correlation—at least in a liberal state—between

9. Lynn M. Festa, *Sentimental Figures of Empire in Eighteenth-
Century Britain and France* (Baltimore, 2006).

10. Bass, *Freedom's Battle*, pp. 342, 5.

11. Ibid., p. 375; compare Karen Halttunen, "Humanitarianism
and the Pornography of Pain in Anglo-American Culture," *American
Historical Review* 100, no. 2 (1995): 303–4.

press coverage, meaningful compassion and beneficent intervention. Remarkably, Bass sidesteps the important debate about the effects of the representation of suffering in words and pictures; he does not grapple at all with the question of whether the daily repetition of sensationalist content can cause "compassion fatigue." Bass's case studies inadvertently illustrate that journalistic coverage of humanitarian crises abroad often trafficked in self-congratulatory rhetoric and racist stereotypes, but he does not account for these shortcomings in his highly idealized portrait of the media. To do so would have wrecked his hypothesis that free states with a free press are by nature well positioned to promote humanity abroad.

The second syndrome is that humanitarians have been drawn in by the spectacle of blood, with the structural causes of the violence, and the consequences of intervention, exciting less emotion. Humanitarianism has not opposed suffering universally; most often, it has fastened on extravagant bodily violation and pain. Again, the Christian roots of modern pity—with Jesus' Passion, not to mention confessional boundaries, setting the terms of emotional identification—are clear here. For this reason, torture, slavery, atrocity and (more recently) rape have gotten humanitarian attention. Then as now, humanitarianism ended up revealing explosive spectacles of suffering at the price of concealing their political, social and cultural conditions, including Western involvement in it. Vivid imagery beamed from far away—like stories sent by telegraph in an earlier era—leaves the misleading impression that you are not already there. Victorians were not troubled by such dilemmas because they assumed that peoples of other cultures, or colors, were simply prone to inhumanity. We are not Victorians, yet Bass seems uninterested in why the "way of the world," with all its inequalities in suffering, was the way it was—and why it is the way it is. All of Bass's showcase episodes are more the prisoner of this syndrome than they are analyses of it: they begin with sketchy political background, then turn to the main event of "the massacre" in order to reach the point of necessary aid.

Third, sentimentalism was profoundly selective, not just in the kinds of problems it targeted but also in the types of people who deserved pity. Sometimes concern about distant atrocities screened out the suffering of those closer to home. In a chapter of *Bleak House* called "Telescopic Philanthropy," Charles Dickens writes about a prim humanitarian named Mrs. Jellyby, who decries distant suffering to the skies while remaining oblivious to the family chaos under her roof.[12] Similarly, when premier humanitarian Florence Nightingale broke the hearts of the British with her appeal to help suffering soldiers during the Crimean War (at least, those on their side), a skeptic asked, "If the veil had been lifted up here [in London] from the last two months of cholera and the whole truth had been told about the sufferings of the poor in their ill-provided dwellings a picture far more harrowing even than that from Constantinople might easily have been drawn. But *cui bono?*" Of course, helping one person always involves ignoring another, but neither in humani-tarianism until recently nor in Bass's book is the itinerary to the latest massacre compared with the road not taken.

Even within the domain of foreign policy and high politics, humanitarian identification happened selec-tively, as Bass cannot help but show. Though all of his

---

12. For the historical basis for this episode, see Howard Temperley, *White Dreams, Black Africa: The Antislavery Expedition to the River Niger 1841–1842* (New Haven, 1991), especially the Epilogue.

case studies are about Christians beset by Muslims (and Druse, in the case of Syria), Bass circles round in the end to implying that there was no tight correlation between Christianity and compassion during the nineteenth century. His argument loses its moorings, however, as he struggles with the impossible mission of bracketing Gladstone's Christian vision of the world order. Given the considerable evidence his book provides that the Christian identity of the victims mattered to humanitarians, the few other cases Bass can cite are the proverbial exceptions that confirm the rule.[13] He insists that the cause of British identification with the Greeks was not their Christianity but some sense of connection between the Greek origins of Western civilization and the present Greek cause, as if this argument made the identification less selective. By and large, atrocities in the nineteenth century were those committed by other (sorts of) people. This makes it an odd period in which to locate the breakthrough to the post-imperialist morality of the "responsibility to protect" today. In the end it is puzzling why Bass takes Victorian solicitude for humanity so seriously, when his book proves Victorians never saw humanity beyond the fringes of Europe—except, of course, when they proclaimed the need to bring European civilization there.

Finally, sentimentalist politics—including humanitarian intervention—can be profoundly diversionary from the real workings of power, or even provide it with new pretexts for its deployment. No one can doubt that it speaks well of humanitarian activists in a post-Holocaust era that they call for the defense of the innocent

---

13. Rodogno, *Against Massacre*, is especially clear on this point, making the entanglement of humanitarian intervention with the so-called Eastern question, rather than a theory about its initiation by liberal states still committed to empire, his fundamental framework.

abroad against outrageous treatment. Usually, however, Western statesmen who advocate for intervention to combat atrocity are embroiled in a more complicated game, as Bass often stresses. In the nineteenth century, the game was the famous "Eastern question," and its prize, not always formal, of course, was control of the Ottoman borderlands. Often, things are more complex on the ground, even when (as in Darfur today) local struggle is so lopsided that counterinsurgency slides into genocide. Sentimentalism, which teaches you to see "humanity," often obscures a knottier politics of nationality or ethnicity. It has become a regular occurrence that after powerful outsiders intervene to restrain killing, the victims typically angle not for universal rights but for local power grabs. Jeremy Harding, for example, suggests that the diminishment of the West's sentimental investment in Kosovo, combined with local dynamics and festering grievances, have practically guaranteed that political parochialism, along with economic stagnation, poverty and graft, will prevail there.[14] Bass's Victorian case studies show that the plight of the suffering could not be separated from overarching imperial rivalries and awakening national sentiments, but tellingly, his stories tail off after the atrocity is put down. In sum, humanitarian myopia screens out a lot of local dynamics from a crisis, the better to wade into it with heartfelt compassion but deplorable ignorance.

None of these syndromes seem real when you are in their grip. Humanitarians are often tempted—Bass certainly is—to believe that anyone doubtful about their politics is simply lazy or immoral. He claims that liberals are the

---

14. Jeremy Harding, "Saved and Depoliticised at One Stroke," *London Review of Books*, July 17, 2008.

only ones who really care about the suffering, and that progressives who worry about the global ramifications of humanitarian causes as well as the local dynamics of an intervention and its potential political impact end up closely resembling conservatives who argue for non-interventionist restraint. "Realism," Bass reports, "aligns with radical leftism."[15] But critics and skeptics who highlight the shortcomings of humanitarianism may have more suffering, not less, in their sights.

As a history written after the fall of communism, Bass's tale neglects perhaps the most important point about humanitarianism, which is that there have been many alternative versions of it. Through the twentieth century, indeed, it was not liberal but leftist humanitarianism that most appealed to the "wretched of the earth," for these had good reason to be suspicious of Western "solidarity." But my point is not that what the suffering have desired is obviously more plausible. It is the more disquieting possibility that humanitarianism, while universal in its rhetoric, has always turned out to be a specific political project in practice. If this interferes with the search for a glorious tradition, perhaps the search makes no sense. All the same, nineteenth-century history teaches that many people desired a version of humanitarianism beyond the form they knew.

And we should sympathize, for we have not even begun to think about how to save compassion from its perversions. Ultimately, the deep past provides little guidance for thinking about how to reform humanitarianism, except for the all-important starting point of its syndromes. For his part, Bass brackets and qualifies suspect motives in order to make the balance sheet work out, and he is comfortable with a humanitarianism that

15. Bass, *Freedom's Battle*, p. 15.

was and remains the creature of great-power politics, with all that entails. Moralizing the great powers, as Bass wants to do, risks glamorizing them. If humanitarian moralizing does not go further, and simply accepts the way of the world that makes humanitarianism necessary, then it is bound to be unconvincing: a spoonful of idealistic sugar will not make the medicine of power go down.

But perhaps it is wrong to read *Freedom's Battle* as a study of the nineteenth century, since a closer look suggests it is really about the last decade of the twentieth century and the early years of the twenty-first. Like Samantha Power, Bass started out his career as a journalist galvanized, after the rise of Holocaust memory, by the outbreak of atrocities in the Balkans in the 1990s. He is now a trained political scientist, and he is officially concerned with combating what in his discipline is called realism, with Benjamin Disraeli, Gladstone's nemesis, taking the role of Henry Kissinger. But the animating spirit of Bass's book appears to be not so much any professional agenda as it is the desire to vindicate the model of moral engagement of a whole generation. The model is one in which, when idealistic activism succeeds, an outraged public begs for defense of the suffering, and great power (eventually) responds. As an *apologia pro vita nostra*, Bass's book is intended to vindicate those who burn with moral passion and believe that they selflessly want only to protect innocents from slaughter, even to the point that they need to pressure a powerful state to bring itself (and its armies) to bear. Humanitarians "just want to resist atrocity," Bass maintains.[16]

A decade ago, more than a few liberal hawks were

16. Ibid., p. 379.

impressed enough by that model to invoke it as a rationale for invading Iraq and destroying Saddam Hussein's rape rooms and torture chambers (to use the rhetoric of the day). Some humanitarian defenders of the Iraq aggression, having soiled their reputations by mistakenly depicting it as "freedom's battle," have simply apologized—as Michael Ignatieff did in 2007 in an embarrassingly vacuous piece in *The New York Times Magazine*.[17] Bass's position is that he was never fooled into believing Iraq counted as a humanitarian cause. "The promotion of human rights was a side benefit," he explains. ("It weighed more heavily in the minds of some of the war's backers," he admits.) In other words, Bass insists that if you choose your humanitarian causes wisely, and really mean to help, there will not be anything to be sorry about.[18]

You will, of course, have to tread carefully, and Bass claims that the nineteenth century is helpful here, too, for policy wonks boning up for the next humanitarian mission. It shows, he claims, "how the practice of humanitarian intervention can be *managed*."[19] Briefly, you only consider intervening when you know you will not ignite a tinderbox; then you make sure to forge a multilateral consensus and do everything you can to avoid the appearance of ulterior motives; finally, you get out as soon as possible.

The first part of the prescription involves a healthy incorporation of realism, leading to the paradoxical consequence that Bass advocates intervention only for those victims whose executioners are not powerful enough to repel or complicate a humanitarian mission,

---

17. Michael Ignatieff, "Getting Iraq Wrong," *New York Times Magazine*, August 5, 2007.

18. Bass, *Freedom's Battle*, p. 379.

19. Ibid., p. 360.

or who are not protected by those powerful enough to do so. Bass shies away from proclaiming the "responsibility to protect," which seemed, a few short years ago, to be the emerging norm of the humanitarian ethos; here he illustrates, once again, that he advocates a moralist's tweak to great-power cynicism rather than a full-scale alternative to it.

The clearest example of the prescription's multilateral element is Bass's case study of the French-initiated intervention in Syria in 1860. After Maronite Christians joined a civil war against their Druse neighbors, the Ottomans, who sided with the Druse (many Muslims joined in the killing), failed to put the lid back on the crisis. When the French public went berserk, demanding action after local Christians and their missionaries died, the British stayed calm. With their greater liberalism and freer press, Bass explains, the British could see this conflict in more even-handed terms. But after some hesitation, the British did play a role, especially in the diplomacy of the intervention, and they prevented the French from treating the cause of humanity as a pretext for a land grab.

As interesting as the case is, it feels like instrumental history. It's not just that Bass's other cases do not work as well. During the 1990s, when Samantha Power and others treated multilateralism as a recipe for inaction, the implication was that the United States might need to act alone, without the sanction of the UN, to stop atrocities, a view Power codified in *"A Problem from Hell."* Power's later biography of Sergio Vieira de Mello, *Chasing the Flame*, now extols multilateralism as a device for obtaining legitimacy.[20] Bass's history

---

20. Samantha Power, *Chasing the Flame: Sergio Vieira de Mello and the Fight to Save the World* (New York, 2008).

reflects this learning, with the nineteenth century presented as an era when the great powers struck the right balance between multilateral consent and unilateral leadership. But one is left with the question of why history matters if the lessons you call on it to teach simply affirm the policy wisdom you actually reached by living through disaster.

What has clearly survived the Iraq debacle is belief not just in anyone's leadership but in the United States' especially. When Bass surveys American history, he exempts the country from the purely European practice of pursuing empire in the name of humanity. He even labels the tail end of the nineteenth century, when the United States began nibbling at Spain's old imperial possessions (much the way Europeans had done with the Ottoman fringes), a "period of imperial temptation" only.[21] Is this remotely plausible? Either way, it's clear that Americans have shown themselves since that time to be quick studies in Victorian rhetoric: "We unsheathed the sword . . . in the name of humanity," as Senator (and future President) Warren Harding described the Cuban invasion of 1898 in retrospect, "and we gave proof to the world at that time of an unselfish nation."[22] In his chapters on the United States, however, Bass chooses to fault the country only for the sin of inaction, saddled as it was by politicians, from John Quincy Adams to Woodrow Wilson, who failed to act on the humanitarian solidarity that the country's constitutional liberalism and free press should have required, at least according to Bass's theory. (Of course, the same held true of the liberal

21. Bass, *Freedom's Battle*, p. 346.
22. Cited in Stowell, *Intervention*, p. 121.

West during the Holocaust, whose memory is so important to current calls for humanitarian intervention.[23])

Even if you think the problem is inaction, you have to treat the risks of calls for humanitarian intervention as seriously as you do the complacency you allege in those who do not sign up. It's misleading to reduce the ethos of humanitarian intervention to the mission in Iraq, but that does not mean they were entirely unrelated. Bass points out that Saddam would have been taken down even if many humanitarians had not joined in the call for blood—which they certainly did. Even so, their support contributed to the public legitimacy of America's war at a crucial moment, and for a depressingly long time.

As much as humanitarian collusion in the Iraq debacle, the use of compassion as a language of international politics, which exploded during the 1990s, is in dire need of re-examination. You may protest that you meant well when you unsheathed the sword. But the sword is double-edged, never more so than when someone who lacks your good intentions gets to swing it.[24]

---

23. See Tony Kushner, *The Holocaust and the Liberal Imagination: A Social and Cultural History* (New York, 1995); for a recent and nuanced picture, Richard Breitman and Allan J. Lichtman, *FDR and the Jews* (Cambridge, MA, 2013).

24. Bass has responded with not a little skepticism to my approach to the history of human rights. See Bass, "The Old New Thing," the *New Republic*, October 20, 2010.

4

OF DESERTS AND PROMISED LANDS: ON INTERNATIONAL COURTS

When people imagine global justice, most often they picture a courtroom. In some ways the image is very old. According to the Hebrew Bible, God's rule requires that the judges man the gates of civilization; at the climax of Aeschylus' *Oresteia*, Athens abandons the vengeful justice of the old gods for the civic accountability of courts. Despite these ancient sources, however, today's dream is also radically new. Where courts once palliated fears that our unbridled actions would have terrible consequences unless governed by law, they now foster hopes for the compensation of wrongs suffered by people in faraway lands. Created a decade ago, the International Criminal Court (ICC) enjoys the highest possible jurisdiction to enforce global morality, a step beyond the nation-state toward truly universal justice.

Advocates of the judicial vision of global justice say they are out to "end impunity," but their recent prominence follows from more than pristine hope. The rise of international criminal accountability has occurred alongside the eclipse of prior schemes of global justice, which promoted not retributive punishment but social renovation to achieve liberty and equality. This aspiration had old roots too. The dream of collective redemption pulsed through prophetic Judaism, and in *The Republic* Plato announced a vision of justice that prizes not merely the avoidance of tyranny but achieving the good life for society.

This agenda—a constructive rather than merely corrective one—became common in modern states when democratic norms and economic circumstances made hierarchy intolerable and social transformation feasible. As global humanity sought the freedom promised by modern times, the dream of social renewal also became internationalized beyond tribe, city and state. This occurred long before anybody called for the establishment of an international criminal court. During the Cold War competition between welfarist and communist visions of democracy, the dream of social renewal was at the fore; now it has mostly vanished at home and abroad. At best, what remains are minor remedies for the amelioration of the worst sort of suffering. Meanwhile, judges and courts have become our fixation. How has international criminal justice ascended so quickly, and so high, even as social justice is increasingly marginalized, undermined from within at home and eroded through the victory of the free market on the world stage?

In *The Slave Trade and the Origins of International Human Rights Law*, Jenny Martinez does not address this question.[1] Her interesting account of how international courts were invented to mitigate the Atlantic slave

---

1. Jenny S. Martinez, *The Slave Trade and the Origins of International Human Rights Law* (New York, 2011).

trade entirely skirts it. But the story was certainly worth telling. True, these "mixed commissions," created by Great Britain with various treaty partners and in operation mainly from the 1820s through the 1840s, are a minor episode in the overall history of the abolition of human bondage. Yet Martinez, concluding that they have been unfairly excluded from what she calls "the international human rights law narrative," gives them the attention they deserve in our time of achieving humanity through courts.

Her description of how the mixed commissions worked is useful indeed. Britain's prohibition of the slave trade in 1807 applied only to its own country's ships. During the next few years, as its war with Napoleon raged, Britain began seizing vessels flying enemy flags to ascertain if they were carrying slaves; if so, they released the slaves, auctioned the ship and awarded part of the proceeds to the captor, rules that had long been part of international custom. But with Napoleon's fall and the war's end, it became much more legally dubious to stop, search, and capture ships.

Britain renewed its enforcement of abolition on the high seas by signing bilateral treaties with various powers whose vessels sailed the Atlantic. The treaties held that both sides could search ships for slaves and remove offenders to special international courts, where judges typically released the slaves and awarded the ship as a finder's fee. France never entered the system of bilateral treaties, and the United States did so only during its Civil War, exceptions that created considerable loopholes: by flying French or American colors, any ship could transport slaves without risk. Never in this era did slavers become the "enemies of mankind" that pirates had long been considered by consensus.[2] All the same, the treaty arrangements led many Africans otherwise destined for New World slavery to be released, chiefly in the British colony of Sierra Leone. Over time, the courts, which also operated in Havana and elsewhere, tried the cases of 600 captured vessels and released 80,000 human beings from chattel slavery. Judged against the vast reach and volume of the slave trade, which transported over ten million human beings for bondage, the attempt to interdict it through international courts was negligible. And many slaves died during the weeks or months it could take to sail captured ships to court. But for those 80,000 human beings, the interdiction made all the difference in the world.

Martinez's description of this victory, however, is more useful than her analysis of it. A Stanford law professor who helped argue *Rumsfeld v. Padilla* before the US Supreme Court, Martinez hopes to bolster contemporary human rights law by claiming that it was formed in the battle against slavery and consequently has already made a great difference to the world. With her single-minded focus, Martinez ends up telling an uplifting story with many blind spots. For example, she admits to being unsure why countries with much to gain from maintaining the trade were motivated to sign bilateral treaties with

---

2. This fact is interesting in view of the mistaken belief by American judges in Alien Tort Statute cases—from *Filártiga v. Peña-Irala* (1980) forward—that the example of pirates provided the basis of a universal jurisdiction extended to slavers under international law. For further details on the evolution of the category of *hostis humani generis*, see Dan Edelstein, *The Terror of Natural Right: Republicanism, the Cult of Nature, and the French Revolution* (Chicago, 2009), Prologue; Daniel Heller-Roazen, *The Enemy of All: Piracy and the Law of Nations* (New York, 2009), and Eugene Kontorovich, "The Piracy Analogy: Universal Jurisdiction's Hollow Foundation," *Harvard International Law Journal* 45, no. 1 (Winter 2004): 183–237.

Britain. More troublingly, she also ignores Britain's complicated motivations, simply assuming that pure benevolence led it to establish the international courts.

As New York University historian Lauren Benton has shown, however, the British government shouldered this costly interdiction effort in order to cement its imperial control of the oceans. The same was true of the separate attempts by some nations—though not the United States—to declare slavers enemies of mankind and thus, like pirate ships, open to boarding and capture even outside the system of bilateral treaties. (Martinez supplements her account of the mixed commissions with coverage of this tactic.) That the British Empire proved open to humanitarian voices at home was not so much a case of power bending to morality as of morality bending to power. Humanity provided the warrant for what one observer acidly called "war in disguise," when in an age of rival empires the policing of the seas was crucial.[3]

As if writing history were a game of connect the dots, Martinez soon leaves the nineteenth century behind, attempting to show that mixed commissions inspired later activism in international law. Her struggle to prove this proposition betrays the flimsiness of her evidence. Martinez insightfully claims that the attack on the slave trade was the first instance in which international law allowed for the

---

3. For the argument and citation, see Lauren Benton, "Abolition and Imperial Law, 1780–1820," *Journal of Imperial and Commonwealth History* 39, no. 3 (2011): 355–74. The point is most definitely not that no abolitionists had defensible or even praiseworthy motives, but rather that the socio-historical conditions in which they make a difference also have to be investigated. It cannot possibly be right to think that merely positing pure motives somewhere is sufficient intellectually to defend a result. Compare Jenny Martinez, "Human Rights and History," *Harvard Law Review Forum* 126 (2013): 221–40, which incorporates a response to this chapter.

protection of non-citizens abroad, though it did not pioneer accountability for individual slavers (except through the loss of their ships and property). But sometimes inspiring precedents are forgotten, and the fact that Martinez needed to excavate this one undermines her case for its legacy as a well-worn "bridge to the future."

Martinez's book is part of a larger trend among historians to reclaim abolition for the sake of today's human rights agenda in all its controversial specifics. Nobody doubts that abolition was a good cause and restored the humanity of those it helped. But there is still an essential debate to have about whether the fight against slavery undergirds the principles and actions of today's international human rights regimes and movements. Of course, nobody in the nineteenth century ever proposed a larger international plan to try criminals, whether for slaving or anything else.

In fact, abolitionists very rarely used the idea of rights, activated as they more typically were by Christianity, humanitarianism or other ideologies. The availability of a natural rights paradigm has long had a place in the history of antislavery.[4] But there is no way to invoke it without specifying its comparative relevance in view of other discourses, a relevance that waxed and waned over time.[5] More important, given the right to private property in natural law, rights talk easily cut in the direction of slavery, rather than against it.[6] In the

---

4. David Brion Davis, *The Problem of Slavery in Western Culture* (Ithaca, 1966), especially Chapter 14.

5. Cf. Martinez, "Human Rights and History," for confident but unsubstantiated assertion of the general relevance and overall prominence of rights talk.

6. Compare William Palmer, "How Ideology Works: Ideology and the Case of British Abolitionism," *Historical Journal* 52, no. 4 (December 2009): 1039–51 at 1049–50.

United States, it is even true that abolitionists for a brief period in the 1830s invoked "human rights," but this practice waned. In more transnational activism around slavery through the nineteenth century, rights were rarely central. Most embarrassingly, in international law, natural rights as a basis for freedom were entirely absent.[7] In spite of the novel though indirect effect of the mixed commissions on the protection of non-citizens, it matters greatly that neither in practice nor in theory did they confer any rights on slaves (especially not legal rights based on their humanity).[8]

And as much as everyone admires abolitionism, it is equally clear that the cause immediately served many political enterprises, manumission being just one. Most of all, abolition burnished Britain's moral credentials as it gobbled up foreign territory after establishing mastery of the seas. The legacy of abolition in international law was primarily a colonialist one, as with the Berlin treaty of 1885, when the great powers carved up Africa among themselves. The heartstrings were tugged by promises of humanitarian campaigns, with the treaty's European signatories vowing to "watch over the preservation of the native tribes, and to care for the improvement of the conditions of their moral and material well-being, and to help in suppressing slavery, and especially the Slave

---

7. Compare Martinez, *The Slave Trade*, pp. 135–9.

8. For this reason, the obvious internationalism of the commissions, on which Martinez rightly lays stress, needs to be connected to their equally obvious failure to extend legal or other rights to slaves. Indeed, it seems crucial to me that what (little?) incidence of natural rights claims there was in antislavery generally did not carry over at all to international law for a very long time, either in the specific case of the commissions or any other setting. See, again, Martinez, "Human Rights and History," as well as Philip Alston, "Does the Past Matter? On the Origins of Human Rights," *Harvard Law Review* 126, no. 5 (May 2013): 2043–81.

Trade."[9] W. E. H. Lecky famously called abolition "among the three or four perfectly virtuous pages comprised in the history of nations," and Martinez similarly needs it to be an unqualified good in order to trade on its legacy.[10] She writes in passing that colonialism remains "controversial," but does not say anything else about it. Even more disturbing, she says the lesson of her history is that international law, great power and military force should be "mutually beneficial," something she sees as especially relevant now that America faces its last chance to export humanitarianism as its ascendancy wanes, much like Britain's once did.[11]

Even as Martinez fails to mention that British abolitionists rarely resorted to international courts, she only grudgingly admits that slaves freed by abolitionist efforts, especially in Cuba, lived out their lives in penurious circumstances and often forced labor. Such ambiguous consequences of emancipation once caused its students to worry about whether it would lead to new versions of unfreedom.[12] Yet it is also true that after the end of chattel slavery, abolition could prompt novel

9. For the larger intersection of abolitionism and imperialism, see Françoise Vergès, *Abolir l'esclavage, une utopie coloniale: Les ambiguïtés d'une politique humanitaire* (Paris, 2001) and Frédéric Mégret, "Droit international et esclavage: pour une réévaluation," *African Yearbook of International Law,* forthcoming.

10. Earlier literature on abolition was precisely about looking beyond claims like Lecky's, as an obviously false causal explanation. See especially Thomas Bender, ed., *The Antislavery Debate: Capitalism and Abolitionism as a Problem in Historical Interpretation* (Berkeley, 1992), pp. 108, 309 for the Lecky quotation.

11. Martinez, *The Slave Trade,* pp. 154, 166.

12. See, e.g., Thomas C. Holt, *The Problem of Freedom: Race, Labor, and Politics in Jamaica, 1832–1938* (Baltimore, 1992), representative of a whole generation's work in refusing to celebrate antislavery without also considering the real social conditions the triumph of free labor brought about.

insights into how oppression and subjugation still burdened humanity, sometimes in unsuspected forms. That Martinez is the first to think that the legacy of abolition is the campaign for international human rights courts does not cast a shadow on her predecessors; instead, it's mainly proof that partisans of justice—many galvanized by abolition—were pursuing other dreams, causes and mechanisms until yesterday.[13]

In the face of past and continuing debate about the meaning of abolition for future campaigns for justice, Martinez simply assumes it is self-evident that those who admire it should pursue international human rights law in its current forms. But that does not follow in the slightest. Just as a better way to study the past is to understand it in its complexity, it is more convincing to argue a present cause by first determining its political meaning today. Conjuring up a long-past experiment to invigorate the project of international human rights, Martinez risks obscuring the conditions under which the cause of international criminal justice suddenly became so appealing and international courts currently operate. Among other things, for instance, Martinez's stirring story of how Africans were freed thanks to

---

13. In a similar recent book, though he does not go so far as to insist on the origins of universalist law in antislavery, Robin Blackburn considers it a key early framework of the moral notion of human rights itself. But especially when it comes to British humanitarianism and transnational solidarity, the evidence is slight, both in Blackburn's book and in general. Revealingly, Blackburn's writing mainly demonstrates that human rights have become so powerful as a moral framework that even Marxists—who once criticized "bourgeois" rights and formalistic abstraction in general as useless for emancipation—now see no alternative but to recalibrate their politics in terms set by the explosion of human rights in our times. Robin Blackburn, *American Crucible: Slavery, Emancipation, and Human Rights* (New York: Verso, 2011); compare Blackburn, "Reclaiming Human Rights," *New Left Review*, new series 69 (May–June 2011): 126–38.

international law might leave you surprised to learn that the International Criminal Court, which came into being in 2002 in a completely new context, so far has indicted only Africans.

In *The Justice Cascade*, Kathryn Sikkink, a prominent political scientist at the University of Minnesota, offers a somewhat more persuasive historical argument for understanding the ascendancy of international courts.[14] She makes the essential point that these tribunals could not have existed without domestic courts. In particular, during the interregnum between the Nuremberg trials and the establishment of international courts in the 1990s to try Bosnian and Rwandan war criminals, it was local judiciaries that led the charge to hold vile former political leaders accountable.

Sikkink has written one of the most useful books available about the rise of international criminal accountability. She begins by linking its emergence to what Samuel Huntington called, in a celebrated phrase, the "third wave" of democracy, for it was Greece and Portugal that first made use of domestic courts to try former military leaders after their 1974 revolutions. Nations in Latin America soon did the same, first in Argentina after 1983, when Raúl Alfonsín turned to the courts to help move his country beyond its own dictatorial experience. It was in Argentina's courts that Luis Moreno Ocampo, who would become the first chief prosecutor at the ICC, cut his teeth.[15]

Sikkink's argument hits a snag when she philosophizes about what made this venture so influential in

---

14. Kathryn Sikkink, *The Justice Cascade: How Human Rights Prosecutions Are Changing World Politics* (New York, 2011).

15. Ibid., chapters 2–3.

the world, first in Latin America and then globally. Calling on the rebarbative political science theory of "norm diffusion," Sikkink hopes to show that people in local social movements affect actions on the world stage, which is surely true.[16] But like Martinez, Sikkink ignores the darker reasons why morality can shine forth, and why some moralities succeed in attracting powerful backing while others do not. Strangely, she treats power as something that can only deter justice; she says nothing about how power determines which vision of justice prevails.

Her argument is seriously marred because she passes over the ending of Cold War hostilities as the major reason many more states were suddenly willing to flirt with the project of holding leaders to account. She acknowledges that, much like the Nuremberg trials before them, the Greek and Portuguese prosecutions initially had little to no impact on the formation of a transnational judicial agenda. If a movement for international justice began only in the very last years of the Cold War and led to the establishment of the ICC after the Cold War had ended, it was due not so much to "democratization" as to geopolitical change.

In Latin America not least, there had been many different movements for justice throughout the Cold War, and the network of lawyers collaborating with "like-minded states," which Sikkink lauds for pushing the prosecutorial mission, was only one among others. In fact, it was a latecomer to a very specific geopolitical situation. Telling the story of her own career and contacts in engaging set pieces about legal advocacy, Sikkink says she is interested in how norms travel between global and local levels but nowhere admits that

16. Ibid., Part II.

the enterprise of building accountability was driven by elites cooperating across such lines. And the key fact about this set of actors is that—along with human rights movements in general—they achieved their appeal and their access to power in novel circumstances.

The destruction of the Latin American left, along with the fall of its counter-revolutionary enemies, was the context in which "transitional justice" became a substitute idealism for many trying to invigorate new democratic regimes in the final years of the Cold War and immediately after.[17] Whether it was an inspiring project depends entirely on what alternatives you think there were, not simply for worse but also for better. In the beginning, for Alfonsín, the prosecutions were linked to a much broader vision of justice, yoking the retrospective and corrective to the futuristic and constructive.[18] But ultimately, the end of the Cold War made some dreams illusory and others plausible far beyond Latin America. Sikkink's "cascade" metaphor for understanding the accountability trend obscures these facts.

Anyway, I am not sure it is a credit to justice to describe it as spreading in the same way that—in the Malcolm Gladwell anecdote Sikkink says she is drawing on—Hush Puppies went from being uncool to ultrachic.[19] More important, the metaphor of a cascade suppresses the human insight and opportunity involved in pursuing justice. Humans are not water: with our ideologies and interests, norms spread among us because of choice and circumstance. And we always have more

---

17. See, brilliantly, Paige Arthur, "How 'Transitions' Reshaped Human Rights: A Conceptual History of Transitional Justice," *Human Rights Quarterly* 31, no. 2 (May 2009): 321–67.

18. Consider Owen M. Fiss, *The Dictates of Justice: Essays on Law and Human Rights* (Dordrecht, 2011).

19. Sikkink, *Justice Cascade*, p. 12.

than one ideology—more than one possible vision of justice—to pursue, so a cascade for one is a dam for another.[20] Sikkink admits to having doubts about her scheme when she insists that "diffuse" is an active verb in her lexicon.[21] Besides failing to note that elites drove the project of spreading the goal of accountability, she does not see that elites were able to make their project stick only when other schemes of justice—ones that had previously been more aspirational and more popular—had been made unavailable or unexciting. One stream seemed major only as earlier torrents evaporated. Elite networks surely mattered, but only in a story about great-power conflict and shifting ideology.

If so, and not least when it comes to Latin America, Sikkink should have begun with the premise that the "justice cascade" of international criminal accountability was in the first instance a selection among or narrowing of the potential meanings of justice. Its goal was not to change society from top to bottom, as many Latin Americans had earlier hoped, but to punish those who—as in the case of the Chilean general, Augusto Pinochet—had risen to power to eliminate the possibility of social reform.

Examining the practical difference prosecutions make, Sikkink honestly acknowledges that the jury is still out on whether individual criminal accountability improves the world, even if just to prevent the sorts of abuses for which courts put individuals on trial. Then she turns to an even tougher question: whether the most powerful nation in the world, the United States, can remain

---

20. For further thoughts, see "On the Non-Globalization of Ideas," in Samuel Moyn and Andrew Sartori, eds, *Global Intellectual History* (New York, 2013).

21. Sikkink, *Justice Cascade*, p. 250.

permanently outside the practices of retroactive justice that Sikkink sees as increasing around the globe.[22]

In one sense, the answer is obvious. The United States has not ratified the treaty forming the ICC, so its leaders cannot be prosecuted by it. Nevertheless, Sikkink contends that because the US government is party to an array of international legal instruments (notably the Convention against Torture, of which she gives a useful account), lawyers in the George W. Bush administration felt compelled to consider potential international accountability for the mistreatment of detainees. Most notoriously, Bush's legal adviser John Yoo offered up "torture memos" explaining that the prohibition of torture by various international treaties applied to some practices but not others. The documents were abhorrent. But as Sikkink observes, had all the president's men not feared punishment under future circumstances, they would not have defined torture down, or granted CIA requests for cards to get out of jail free.

Converting what might seem like an objection to her case into an argument for it, Sikkink's account of the torture memos is ingenious and probably right; but it does not then follow that American power is under significant threat from international law, or that Bush is going to be put on trial anytime soon. Not long ago Amnesty International asked Canada to arrest and try him during a planned visit there, but Canadian officials dismissed the request as a stunt. Though more than a trickle, the calls for international criminal accountability for human rights abuses will ring hollow so long as the powerful remain high and dry, as Sikkink should have more clearly acknowledged. Not having recognized America's Cold War victory as the geopolitical

22. Ibid., Part III.

context for the rise of one vision of justice as opposed to others, Sikkink cannot fully reckon with the coincidence that America has been left out of that very trend so far—except as sometimes beneficent helper when the Court's agenda coincides with the country's.

All the same, while the least promising fact about Martinez's account of mixed commissions is that the greatest power in the world ran them, it is to Sikkink's credit that she is openly nervous about the glaring difficulty of international criminal tribunals: originally promoted by lesser nations, the ICC has become a forum for accusing their leaders alone. Sikkink's prediction that one day the United States will be flooded with calls for international justice is wildly optimistic, and her focus on regions other than Africa leaves the politics of international criminal law unclear, given that it is most concentrated and most enigmatic on that continent.

If the remote and recent past of international criminal justice is too complicated to narrate as a fairy tale, its current and future possibilities are ultimately hazy. International courts may not be a mirage, but one thing is clear. They emerged as an oasis because people had stopped searching for a promised land where the fight for equity involves more than litigating past crime. Many people who in modern times have answered to the name liberal or progressive, far from preferring courts as agents of change, have fought in public for the elimination of unfair divisions of wealth and power. These have been the ultimate causes of misery at home, as well as in a self-evidently unjust international order. Indicting, trying, and convicting fallen despots, though a highly political act domestically or across borders, can undoubtedly serve justice.

But it is not wrong to ask how much, and at what cost to other battles for justice.

Sikkink says forthrightly that the "cascade" to which she refers leaves aside justice in some larger and reconstructive sense, suggesting simply that it has become increasingly legitimate—though not inevitable—for individual statesmen to be put on trial in the wake of atrocious wrongs of state. But a different tradition will have to be rediscovered if justice is to move from overcoming crimes of the past to debating plans for the future, whether they involve a better state or a defensible global order.

It is here that the rise of the international court in the idealistic imagination is particularly significant, for it is obvious that strong and wealthy nations are never going to legally mandate their own loss of superiority and money—and no court will dare call them enemies of mankind for not doing so. For her part, Martinez permits herself to dream for a moment when she suggests that her story might someday help us see that the powerless and poor of the world need our help just as the slaves once did. Then she checks herself: "To be sure, few if any of these problems are susceptible to resolution by international courts."[23] True enough, but then the reason to study their past and present ought to be not just to register their heroic possibilities but also to acknowledge their humbling limitations.

---

23. Martinez, *The Slave Trade*, p. 165.

5

HUMAN RIGHTS IN HISTORY

Only a few decades ago, on January 20, 1977, Jimmy Carter inaugurated his presidency by proclaiming from the Capitol steps, "Because we are free we can never be indifferent to the fate of freedom elsewhere... Our commitment to human rights must be absolute."[1] Most people had never heard of "human rights." Except for Franklin Delano Roosevelt in a couple of passing references, no president had really mentioned the concept, and it never had gained much traction around the world either. Carter's words sparked an intense debate at every level of government and society, and in political capitals across the Atlantic Ocean, about what it would entail to shape a foreign policy based on the principle of human rights.

The concept of rights, including natural rights, stretches back centuries, and "the rights of man" were a centerpiece of the age of democratic revolution. But those *droits de l'homme et du citoyen* meant something different from today's "human rights." For most of modern history, rights have been part and parcel of battles over the meanings and entitlements of

---

1. Jimmy Carter, Inaugural Address, January 20, 1977.

citizenship, and therefore have been dependent on national borders for their pursuit, achievement and protection. In the beginning, they were typically invoked by a people to found a nation-state of their own, not to police someone else's. They were a justification for state sovereignty, not a source of appeal to some authority—like international law—outside and above it.

In the United States, rights were also invoked to defend property, not simply to defend women, blacks and workers against discrimination and second-class citizenship. The New Deal assault on laissez-faire required an unstinting re-examination of the idea of natural rights, which had been closely associated with freedom of contract since the nineteenth century and routinely defended by the Supreme Court. By the 1970s, rights as a slogan for democratic revolution seemed less pressing, and few remembered the natural rights of property and contract which the New Deal had once been forced to challenge. Carter was free to invoke the concept of rights for purposes it had never before served. (Arthur Schlesinger Jr. once called on future historians to "trace the internal discussions . . . that culminated in the striking words of the inaugural address." No one, however, yet knows exactly how they got there.)[2]

It looks like Carter was an exception in another sense. He inaugurated the era of human rights in this country, but now it seems to be fading. Bill Clinton dabbled in human rights while outlining a new post–Cold War foreign policy, but the Democratic politician now in the White House has spurned them. Few developments seem

---

2. Arthur M. Schlesinger, Jr., "Human Rights and the American Tradition," in *The Cycles of American History* (New York, 1986), pp. 97–8; but cf. now Barbara J. Keys, *Reclaiming American Virtue: The Human Rights Revolution of the 1970s* (Cambridge, MA, 2014), for the authoritative study.

more surprising than the fact that Barack Obama rarely mentions human rights, especially since past enthusiasts for them like Samantha Power and Anne-Marie Slaughter have major roles in his foreign policy shop. Obama has given no major speech on the subject and has subordinated the concerns associated with human rights, such as taking absolute moral stands against abusive dictators, to a wider range of pragmatic foreign policy imperatives. As his Nobel remarks made plain, Obama is a "Christian realist" inclined to treat human sin, not human rights, as the point of departure for thinking about America's relation to the world's many injustices and horrors.

The rise and fall of human rights as an inspirational concept may seem shocking, but perhaps it is less so on second glance. Ever since Carter put human rights on the table, Republican presidents have found uses for them too, typically by linking them to "democracy promotion" abroad. There is no denying the powerful growth of non-governmental organizations in the United States and around the world that has occurred since slightly before Carter's time, and impressively ever since. But George W. Bush, placing himself in an almost equally longstanding tradition, invoked human rights as the battle cry for the neoconservative vision of transforming the Middle East and beyond—at the point of a gun, if necessary—perhaps sullying them beyond recuperation. Obama seems to think so. If their current abeyance is surprising, perhaps it's because of a historical mistake: the belief that human rights were deeply ingrained in American visions of the globe in the first place.

But what about the 1940s, when FDR essentially coined the phrase "human rights" and set in motion a series of events that culminated in the United Nations-sponsored Universal Declaration of Human Rights in 1948? Beginning in the 1990s, when human rights acquired a literally millennial appeal in the public discourse of the West during outbreaks of ethnic cleansing in Southeastern Europe and beyond, it became tempting to treat 1948 as a moment of annunciation, with large political consequences. Carter, and the 1970s, were rarely mentioned. It became common to assume that, ever since their birth in a moment of postgenocidal revulsion and wisdom, human rights had become embedded slowly but steadily in humane consciousness in what amounted to a revolution of moral life. In a euphoric mood, high-profile observers like Michael Ignatieff believed that secure moral guidance, born of incontestable shock about the Holocaust, was on the verge of displacing self-interest and power as the foundation of international relations. In Samantha Power's *"A Problem from Hell,"* Raphael Lemkin, who crafted the draft resolution of the 1948 Convention on the Prevention and Punishment of the Crime of Genocide, was dusted off as a human rights sage and hero, with Carter noted only for failing to intervene against Pol Pot's atrocities.[3]

In fact, when "human rights" entered the English language in the 1940s, it happened unceremoniously, even accidentally. Human rights began as a very minor part of a hopeful alternative vision to set against Adolf Hitler's vicious and tyrannical new order. In the heat of battle and for a short time thereafter, a vision of post-war collective life in which personal freedoms would coalesce with more widely circulating promises of some

---

3. Power, *"A Problem from Hell"*.

sort of social democracy provided the main reason to fight the war.

It's important to enumerate what human rights, in the 1940s, were not. Ignatieff was wrong. They were not a response to the Holocaust, and not focused on the prevention of catastrophic slaughter. Though closely associated with the better life of social democracy, only rarely did they imply a departure from the persistent framework of nation-states that would have to provide it.

Above all, human rights were not even an especially prominent idea. Unlike later, they were restricted to international organization, in the form of the new United Nations. They did not take hold in popular language and they inspired no popular movement. Whether as one way to express the principles of Western postwar societies or even as an aspiration to transcend the nation-state, the concept of human rights never percolated publicly or globally during the 1940s with the fervor it would have in the '70s and the '90s, not even during negotiations over the Universal Declaration.

What if the 1940s were cut loose from the widespread myth that they were a dry run for the post–Cold War world, in which human rights began to afford a glimpse of a rule of law above the nation-state? What if the history of human rights in the 1940s were written with later events given proper credit, and a radically different set of causes for the current meaning and centrality of human rights recaptured? The central conclusion could only be that, however tempting, it is misleading to describe World War II and its aftermath as the essential source of human rights as they are now understood.

From a global perspective, the brief career of human rights in the 1940s is the story of how the Allied nations promoted language about human rights as they reneged on the earlier wartime promise—made in the 1941 Atlantic Charter—of the self-determination of peoples. Global self-determination would have spelled the end of empire, but by war's end the Allies had come around to Winston Churchill's clarification that this promise applied only to Hitler's empire, not empire in general (and certainly not Churchill's). The Atlantic Charter set the world on fire, but because similar language was dropped from the Universal Declaration, human rights fell on deaf ears. It is not hard to understand why. Human rights turned out to be a substitute for what many around the world wanted: a collective entitlement to self-determination. To the extent they noticed the rhetoric of human rights at all, the subjects of empire were not wrong to view it as a consolation prize.

But even when it comes to the Anglo-American, continental European and second-tier states where human rights had at least some minor publicity, the origins of the concept need to be treated within a narrative explaining not their annunciation but their general marginality throughout the mid- to late 1940s. In the beginning, as a vague synonym for some sort of social democracy, human rights failed to address the genuinely pressing question of *which kind* of social democracy to bring about. Should it be a version of welfarist capitalism or a full-blown socialism? A moral language announcing standards above politics offered little at a moment in world history of decisive political choice. By 1947–48 and the crystallization of the Cold War, the West had succeeded in capturing the language of human rights for its crusade against the Soviet Union; the language's main advocates ended up being conservatives on the European continent. Having been too vague to figure in debates about what sort of social democracy to bring about in the mid-1940s, human rights proved soon after to be just another way of arguing for one side in the Cold War struggle. Never at any point were they primarily understood as breaking fundamentally with the world of states that the United Nations brought together.

In considering the origins and peripheral existence of the concept of human rights, the focus should be on the formation of the United Nations, since until not long before Carter's declaration human rights were a project of UN machinery only, along with regionalist initiatives, and had no independent meaning. Yet the founding of the United Nations, and the forging of its Universal Declaration, actually presents a very different storyline from the one imagined by actors in the drama of human rights in the 1990s.

Recall that FDR had to be cajoled into accepting the idea of an international organization. In the Dumbarton Oaks documents—the startling outlines of a prospective international organization for the postwar era discussed by the Allies in 1944—it was clear that the wartime rhetoric that sometimes included the new phrase "human rights" masked the agendas of great-power realism. And the campaign by various individuals and groups up to and during the epoch-making San Francisco conference on the United Nations in mid-1945 to scupper this tactic failed spectacularly, despite the symbolic concession of the reintroduction of the concept of human rights into the charter written there. The victorious wartime alliance had been enshrined as the security council of the new world government, as its seat of true authority, and while some minor states and private citizens attempted to resist a UN that would simply entrench and balance the power of the war's victors, they did not succeed.

If a heroic view of human rights is familiar, it is because

of two common but untenable ways of remembering the period. The first is to overstate—often drastically—the goals and effects of the campaign against the Dumbarton Oaks settlement. The second is to isolate the path toward the Universal Declaration as a road still traveled, even if the Cold War temporarily erected a barrier on it. But instead of a rousing story of how the document emerged against all odds, one needs to tell a less flattering story about why no one cared about it for decades. As an early NGO chief, Moses Moskowitz, aptly observed later, the truth is that human rights "died in the process of being born."[4] Why they were born again for our time is therefore the true puzzle.

The United States, having done so much to drive the global inflation of wartime hopes, quickly retreated from the language it had helped to introduce, leaving Western Europe alone to cultivate it. Even there—especially there—the real debate in domestic politics was about how to create social freedom within the boundaries of the state. Coming after the announcement of the Truman Doctrine in March 1947, with its call for a decisive choice between two "alternative ways of life," the passage of the Universal Declaration in December 1948 offered the mere pretense of unity at a crossroads for humanity. And already by that point, with most emphasis on the right of conscience, European conservatives had captured the language of human rights by deploying it as a synonym for the moral community that secularism (and the Soviets) threatened, while few others learned to speak it.

In any case, "human rights" meant something different in the 1940s. Despite its new international

---

4. Cited in my *Last Utopia*, p. 82.

significance, its core meaning remained as compatible with the modern state as the older tradition of the domestic rights of man had been. Both were the background principles of the nations united by them. In this sense, if in few others, "human rights" preserved a memory of the "rights of man and citizen" more than summoning a utopia of supranational governance through law. The inclusion of social and economic rights in the mid-1940s mattered very much: still relevant rights to economic security and social entitlements were prominent and, unlike today, surprisingly consensual. But they were earlier products of citizenship struggles, and have even now barely affected the international order.

From another viewpoint, however, the postwar moment gave the antique idea of declaring rights an altogether new cast: neither a genuine limitation of prerogative, as in the Anglo-American tradition, nor a statement of first principles, as in the French, the Universal Declaration emerged as an afterthought to the fundamentals of world government it did nothing to affect. No one registered this fact more clearly than the lone Anglo-American international lawyer still campaigning for human rights in 1948, Hersch Lauterpacht, who denounced the Universal Declaration as a shameful defeat of the ideals it grandly proclaimed.

After the 1970s, and especially after the Cold War, it became usual to regard World War II as a campaign for universal justice, with the shock of the discovery of the camps prompting unprecedented commitment to a humane international order. Rather than Moskowitz's story of death in birth, the proclamation of human rights became one of birth after death, especially Jewish death. In the postwar moment itself, however, across weeks of debate around the Universal Declaration in the UN General Assembly, the genocide of the Jews went unmentioned—despite the frequent invocation of other dimensions of Nazi barbarity to justify specific items for protection, or to describe the consequences of leaving human dignity without defense.

The more recent phenomenon of Holocaust memory has also encouraged a mystified understanding of the Nuremberg trials, which in reality contributed to the ignorance of the specific plight of the Jews in the recent war rather than establishing a morally familiar tradition of responding to mass atrocity. The Allies coined the new penal concept of "crimes against humanity" in the days between Hiroshima and Nagasaki, as they wrestled with how to treat the defeated enemy elites. But on the rare occasion the notion referred to the Jewish tragedy, it got short shrift at Nuremberg, at a time when the West knew little and cared less about the Holocaust, and the Soviets wanted patriotic and antifascist victims rather than Jewish ones.

The concept of human rights was not prominently invoked in the proceedings. It is not at all obvious that, at the time, Nuremberg and related legal innovations like the genocide convention were conceived as part of the same enterprise as the itemization of human rights, let alone falling under their umbrella—though they are now often inaccurately described as if they were a single, though multifaceted, achievement. Lemkin, the main force behind the genocide convention, understood his campaign to be at odds with the UN's human rights project. In any case, Lemkin's project was even more marginal and peripheral in the public imagination than the Universal Declaration, passed by the General

Assembly the day after the passage of the genocide resolution.

If there is a pressing reason to return to the history of human rights in the 1940s, it is not because of their importance at the time. The Universal Declaration was less the annunciation of a new age than a funeral wreath laid on the grave of wartime hopes. The world looked up for a moment; then it returned to the postwar agendas that had crystallized at the same time that the United Nations emerged. A better way to think about human rights in the 1940s is to come to grips with why they had no role to play then, compared with the ideological circumstances three decades later, when they made their true breakthrough.

During that interval, two global Cold War visions separated the United States and the Soviet Union, and the rivalry of these visions tore a gash across the European continent. The struggle for the decolonization of empire—movements for the very self-determination that had been scuttled as human rights rose—made the Cold War competition global, even if some new states strove to find an exit from its rivalry to chart their own course. Whereas the American side dropped human rights, both the Soviet Union and anticolonialist forces were committed to collective ideals of emancipation like communism and nationalism as the path into the future. They did not cherish individual rights directly, let alone seek their enshrinement in international law. Utopian ideals were not lacking, but human rights were not one of them.

During the 1960s crisis of superpower order, the domestic consensus in the East and West around the terms of the Cold War began to fracture. Without ever dying in the East, the dream of "building socialism" lost its appeal, while in the West the anxieties of the Cold War and early worries about its costs drove a new generation to depart from the postwar consensus. Yet in the ensuing explosion of dissent, it was not human rights but other utopian visions that prospered. There were calls for community at home to redeem the United States from hollow consumerism; for "socialism with a human face" in the Soviet empire; for further liberation from "neocolonialism" in the Third World. At the time, there were scarcely any non-governmental organizations that pursued human rights; Amnesty International, a fledgling group, remained practically unknown. From the 1940s on, the few NGOs that did include human rights on their agenda worked invisibly and bureaucratically for them within the UN's framework, but their failure over thirty years to become prominent, let alone effective, confirmed the agonizing fruitlessness of this project. As Moskowitz observed bitterly in the early '70s, the human rights idea had "yet to arouse the curiosity of the intellectual, to stir the imagination of the social and political reformer and to evoke the emotional response of the moralist."[5] He was right.

But within one decade, human rights would begin to be invoked across the developed world and by many more ordinary people than ever before. Instead of implying what they had come to mean at the United Nations by the 1960s—further colonial liberation—human rights were used by new forces on the ground, like NGOs, and most often meant individual protection against the state extended by some authority above it. Amnesty International became visible and, as a beacon of new ideals, won the Nobel Peace Prize in 1977—in America, Carter's year—for its work. The popularity of

---

5. Cited in ibid., p. 3.

its mode of advocacy forever transformed the basis for agitating for humane causes, and spawned a brand and age of internationalist citizen engagement.

At the same time, Westerners left the dream of revolution behind, both for themselves and for the Third World they had once ruled, and adopted other tactics, envisioning an international law of human rights as the steward of utopian norms and the mechanism of their fulfillment. Even politicians, Carter towering over them all, started to invoke human rights as the guiding rationale of the foreign policy of states. For Americans, it was a moment of recovery from Henry Kissinger's evil as well as the foreign policy, hatched by Democrats before Kissinger took power, that had led to the Vietnam disaster. After Amnesty won a Nobel Prize, other NGOs began to sprout: Helsinki Watch—now Human Rights Watch—emerged the next year.

Most visible of all, the public relevance of human rights skyrocketed, as measured by the simple presence of the phrase in the newspapers, consolidating the recent supremacy of the notion compared with other schemes of freedom and equality. In 1977 the *New York Times* featured the phrase "human rights" five times more frequently than in any prior year. The moral world had changed. "People think of history in the long term," Philip Roth says in one of his novels, "but history, in fact, is a very sudden thing."[6] Never has this been truer than when it comes to the history of human rights.

But how to explain the recent origins of what now looks like a short-lived faith? The designation of the 1940s as the era when contemporary global commitments were born is one version of a larger mistake. The roots of

---

6. Philip Roth, *American Pastoral* (New York, 1997), p. 87.

contemporary human rights are not to be found where pundits and professors have longed to find them: neither in Greek philosophy nor monotheistic religion, neither in European natural law nor early modern revolutions, neither in horror against American slavery nor Hitler's Judeocide. The temptation to ransack the past for such "sources" says far more about our own time than about the thirty years after World War II, during which human rights were stillborn and then somehow resurrected.

Human rights came to the world in a sort of gestalt switch: a cause that had once lacked partisans suddenly attracted them in droves. While accident played a role in this transformation, as it does in all human events, what mattered most was the collapse of universalistic schemes and the construction of human rights as a persuasive, "moral" alternative to them. These prior universalistic schemes promised a free way of life but led to bloody morass, or offered emancipation from capital and empire but were now felt to be dark tragedies rather than bright hopes. They were the first candidates for replacing the failed premises of the early postwar order, but they failed too. In this atmosphere, an internationalism revolving around individual rights surged. Human rights were minimal, individual and fundamentally moral; not maximal, collective and potentially bloody.

Given its role in the 1940s, the United Nations had to be bypassed as human rights' essential institution for them to matter. The emergence of new states through decolonization, earth-shattering in other respects for the organization, changed the meaning of the very concept of human rights but left it globally peripheral. It was, instead, only in the 1970s that a genuine social movement around human rights made its appearance, seizing the foreground by transcending government institutions, especially international ones. It, too, emphasized that human rights were a moral alternative to the blind alleys of politics.

To be sure, there were a number of catalysts for the explosion: the search for a European identity outside Cold War terms; the reception of Soviet and later Eastern European dissidents by Western politicians, journalists and intellectuals; and the American liberal shift in foreign policy in new, moralized terms, after the Vietnam catastrophe. Equally significant, but more neglected, were the end of formal colonialism and a new view toward the Third World. Empire was foreclosed, yet romantic hopes for decolonization were also smashed and the era of "failed states" was opening.

There is a great irony in the emergence of human rights as the last utopia when others failed. The moral claim to transcend politics that led people to ignore human rights in the 1940s proved to be the cause of the revival and persistence of human rights three decades later, as "ideology" died and the phrase "human rights" entered common parlance. And it is from that recent moment that human rights have come to define the hopes of the present day.

Beyond myth, the true history of human rights matters most of all so that we can confront their prospects today and in the future. A few holdouts aside, progressives have fully adopted human rights into—or even as another phrase for—their politics in the past few decades. And they are correct to do so, since many specific rights, such as principles of equality and well-being, or entitlements to work and education, are those whose content they have defended across modern history. Finally, there is no gainsaying the widespread germination and ambitious agendas of NGOs in the thirty years since human rights came to the fore, most of which attempt pressing changes with the most honorable of intentions. All the same, human rights have to date transformed the terrain of idealism more than they have the world itself.

Moreover, human rights have many faces and multiple possible uses. As much as they call for social concern, they anchor property—the principle of rights having been most synonymous with this protection for most of modern history. They were mobilized in the name of neoconservative "democracy promotion," and have justified liberal warfare and "intervention." They serve as the brand name for diverse schemes of global governance in which vulnerability and inequality persist. What may matter is less the idea of human rights than its interpretations and applications, which are inevitably partisan.

This being the case, why persist in upholding the fiction that human rights name an inviolable consensus everyone shares? Like all universalist projects, human rights are violated every time they are interpreted and transformed into a specific program. Because they promise everything to everyone, they can end up meaning anything to anyone. Human rights have become an ideology—ours—except that, as in the 1940s, it is now difficult to see how the pretense of agreement can help when there is no consensus about how, or even whether, to change the world.

This contemporary dilemma has to be faced squarely; yet history as a celebration of origins will not offer any guidance. To be sure, Obama's "Christian realism" is dubious too, and is no alternative to the human rights mindset of his recent Democratic predecessors. Carter and Obama have been the most assiduous presidential readers of Reinhold Niebuhr, the central Christian realist, who insisted that the reality of sin placed limits on human improvement while requiring great powers like the United States to fight evil (sometimes at the risk of their own besmirchment). But while Carter found in the Protestant divine the courage to indict national sin, Christian realism too often encourages Americans to feel like children of light alone, facing darkness abroad rather than in themselves. Yet Obama's initially surprising caution toward human rights remains useful: it suggests that the faith in the notion may be less deeply rooted than we thought, and not at all indispensable. The real question is what to do with the progressive moral energy to which human rights have been tethered in their short career. Is the order of the day to reinvest it or to redirect it?

In his recent manifesto for a reclaimed social democracy, *Ill Fares the Land*, Tony Judt stirringly calls for a revival of an unfairly scuttled domestic politics of the common good.[7] Judt argues that if the left, after a long era of market frenzy, has lost the ability to "think the state" and to focus on the ways that "government can play an enhanced role in our lives," that's in part because the ruse of international human rights lured it away. The anti-politics of human rights "misled a generation of young activists into believing that, conventional avenues of change being hopelessly clogged, they should forsake political organization for single-issue, non-governmental groups unsullied by compromise."[8] They gave up on political tasks, Judt worries, for the satisfying morality of Amnesty International and other human rights groups.

Whether or not this description is correct, it does not make the retreat to the state as the forum of imagination

7. Tony Judt, *Ill Fares the Land* (New York, 2010).
8. Ibid., pp. 162–4.

and reform seem any more plausible as a next step. After all, mid-century social democracy had its own global context. And today, as Judt points out, "The democratic failure transcends national boundaries."[9] So it is definitely not a matter of choosing the state against the globe, but of deciding how to connect our utopian commitments to make both more just, each goal being the condition of the other. The question remains not whether to have a language and strategy to confront a flawed world beyond our national borders; it is which language and strategy to choose.

One thing is for sure: the lesson of the actual history of human rights is that they are not so much a timeless or ancient inheritance to preserve as a recent invention to remake—or even leave behind—if their program is to be vital and relevant in what is already a very different world than the one into which they erupted. It is up to us whether another utopia should now take the place of human rights, much as they themselves emerged on the ruins of prior dreams.

---

9. Ibid., p. 166.

6

THE INTERSECTION WITH HOLOCAUST MEMORY

How did human rights and the Holocaust get entangled? The purpose of this short reflection, and call for research, is to argue that even to begin answering this question it needs to be framed correctly—as a problem people in the 1940s could not have posed because the entanglement had not yet occurred. What needs to be reckoned with is that it was not the Holocaust in itself that drove the contemporary salience of human rights, but belated memories of it in new circumstances.[1]

Consider a typology of three stages of the conceptual evolution of human rights, starting in the early 1940s. Brutally simplifying, one might label them the welfarist, anticolonial, and humanitarian paradigms in which the coin of human rights was minted and minted again.

It seems fairly clear that the original public meaning of human rights in the 1940s was one synonym for the project of national welfarism whose acceptable forms World War II had been about clarifying. Nobody, after

---

1. See also Andreas Huyssen, "International Human Rights and the Politics of Memory: Limits and Challenges," *Criticism* 53, no. 4 (Fall 2011): 607–24.

1945, was a national socialist anymore in name—but most people believed in the national welfarism that Adolf Hitler had played no small role in bringing to the world, though now with a crucial rhetorical place for personal freedoms.[2] The nation-state exiting patriotic war at the height of its powers was the true victor of World War II, whose politicians justified the war in terms of unprecedented welfarist promises, frequently including economic rights. It was, after all, the welfare state rather than international human rights that World War II was fought to achieve, at least in the framework of consent that politicians garnered for it. The persisting debate was not about the nation-state as the chief forum of collective life, but about whether an acceptable national welfarism would break finally with capitalism. Hence the Cold War that coalesced soon after.

Conversely, from the early 1940s human rights was not yet a concept linked primarily with atrocity, and certainly not with the supranational protection of individuals, which only a few advocated. The simple fact is despite their best efforts historians have found only a tiny number of actors in the 1940s who talked about human rights outside a national welfarist paradigm, focusing instead primarily on the international order generally (aside from envisioning a globalization of national welfarism) or focusing on atrocity prevention specifically. Conversely, in the legal innovations specifically concerned with the regulation of war and characteristically lumped together with the drafting of the Universal Declaration of Human Rights—the Nuremberg trials, the genocide convention, and the

---

2. Consider Wolfgang Schivelbusch, *Three New Deals: Reflections on Roosevelt's America, Mussolini's Italy, and Hitler's Germany, 1933–1939* (New York, 2006).

Geneva conventions—human rights are never mentioned. It was not that the Universal Declaration did not respond to war. But its response presumed that only the national welfarist program would overcome the past, and—unlike contemporaneous documents—did not offer plans for human protection should war return. As a result, the now deeply ingrained assumption that the entire aftermath of World War II, and not least the Universal Declaration, just must have been a response to the Jewish genocide is wrong. Contrary to a generally shared opinion, a cosmopolitan morality based on memory of our emblematic state atrocity did not emerge in the 1940s.

The Universal Declaration does indeed refer to the "disregard and contempt for human rights [that] have resulted in barbarous acts which have outraged the conscience of mankind." This meant that every nation had its horrors, since the Nazis were responsible for many terrible things. The most famous outrages on humanity of the 1940s were Leningrad and Lidice, when Belzec or Treblinka were still unknown. But even to frame the problem this way—in terms of *which atrocities* had pride of place in motivating human rights—seems misguided. One historian, Eric Weitz, has declared that "there is no history of human rights without a history of crimes against humanity."[3] Yet a framework in which historical violence determines their meaning obscures the actual relevance of human rights in the 1940s, centered on their welfarist meaning. For it is that meaning that dominated the phrase on first wartime coinage, before any crimes against humanity had been revealed,

---

3. Eric D. Weitz, "Why It Is Time for a Much More Critical History of Human Rights," *History News Network*, November 22, 2009, historynewsnetwork.com.

and indeed in the most overwhelmingly frequent uses of the idea through the decade.

In any event, for practically no one and for few Jews was the Holocaust, to the extent its enormity was understood at all, the rationale for suprastate law or atrocity prevention directly. If the historiographical goal is to celebrate an international or supranational response to the Holocaust as such in the 1940s, the most vivid example is probably Eastern European antifascism; as for Jews outside the now depopulated "bloodlands," allegiances were won essentially by nationalism at home, in the form of integration, or abroad in the form of often novel Zionist commitments. In their national welfarism, however, Jews were fully in conformity with their times. For everyone else, too, the idea of human rights primarily offered one synonym for the sort of welfarist nation-state that ought to be achieved—with no further search for superordinate constraint, and no specific focus on mass death, genocidal or not.

If so, it is not surprising that in United Nations records it seems that no one—the one possible exception is the likely author of that line about barbarous acts, French Jew René Cassin—had what is now known as the Holocaust of European Jewry in mind as the core meaning of the idea. At least, no diplomats of any nationality mentioned the Holocaust during the yearlong debate around the Universal Declaration. In response to this finding, another historian, Daniel Cohen, has proposed that contemporaries "universalized" their responses to Jewish death in speaking vaguely or humanistically.[4] And it is also true that current historians are pushing

---

4. G. Daniel Cohen, "The Holocaust and the 'Human Rights Revolution': A Reassessment," in Akira Iriye et al., eds., *The Human Rights Revolution: An International History* (New York, 2011).

back against the premise that there was no Holocaust consciousness whatsoever in the immediate postwar years—though it usually turns out the best evidence of its existence is to be found in "private memory" and Jewish subcultures.[5] Without a showing of more pervasive concern in public affairs about the Holocaust, asserting its relevance anyway is a risky proposition, for two reasons. Inferring from something's absence that it was implicit or everywhere does require some sort of evidence. (Most often, when dogs do not bark, it is because they are not there.) Further, to the extent "universalization" happened at all, it has long been alleged that it usually served the purposes of avoidance—especially on a European continent of widespread collaboration and in a world that had turned a blind eye to the horror—rather than acknowledgment. (This connection is not just hypothetical: when it comes to the rise of human rights in European regionalist projects after World War II, Marco Duranti has shown that many reactionaries were involved, who had other purposes in mind than honoring victims.[6])

Most important, however, there is a creditable reason—a reason that many Jews at the time actually shared—for the fact that human rights were not at first

5. For some important examples, see François Azouvi, *Le mythe du grand silence: Auschwitz, les Français, et la mémoire* (Paris, 2012); David Cesarani and Eric J. Sundquist, eds, *After the Holocaust: Challenging the Myth of Silence* (New York, 2011); Hasia Diner, *We Remember with Reverence and Love: American Jews and the Myth of Silence after the Holocaust, 1945–1962* (New York, 2009); Laura Jockusch, *Collect and Record! Jewish Holocaust Documentation in Early Postwar Europe* (New York, 2012). See also my "Silence and the Shoah," *Times Literary Supplement*, August 9, 2013.

6. Marco Duranti, "The Holocaust, the Legacy of 1789, and the Birth of International Human Rights Law," *Journal of Genocide Research* 14, no. 2 (May 2012): 159–86.

defined primarily in terms of atrocity. It's that national welfarism, a constructive political project, seemed like the worthiest response to the past. For people in the 1940s, it seemed most important to put the past behind, or to dwell on it mainly as motivation for a welfarist or otherwise solidaristic alternative to the horrors of aggressive war. This was what the International Military Tribunal at Nuremberg, which certainly was backward-looking, considered of paramount importance, given the overwhelming priority given to the stigmatization of aggressive war over the targeting of atrocity in the proceedings. By and large, criminalizing atrocity had not yet become humanity's fondest hope—a low-level ambition reserved for our time. Instead, national welfarism ruled hearts and minds. If the Universal Declaration was a response to experience, it was essentially to an experience of depression and war, not one of atrocity and genocide, and for the sake of a rapid pivot to building the future.

Now turn to the second, anticolonialist stage. For the fact is that human rights in their first national-welfarist guise had no implications for an end to empire, as indeed the exclusion of self-determination from early human rights ideas—up to and including the Universal Declaration of 1948—shows clearly.

Many had allowed themselves to hope that the world had also been promised decolonization—national welfarism on a global scale—in the Atlantic Charter early in World War II, but Winston Churchill rapidly succeeded in convincing Franklin Roosevelt to demote the promise of self-determination or restrict it to Adolf Hitler's empire, not Churchill's, and human rights rose as self-determination fell. In the second stage of post-war human rights, from the 1950s to the 1970s, global movements to end empire reversed these priorities. Anticolonial human rights followed the national welfarist paradigm but globalized it. And at the high tide of this anticolonial moment, at the United Nations, human rights were successfully defined in terms of the self-determination once deliberately omitted from them. The classic instances of this, in international politics, are UN General Assembly Resolutions 1514 (1960) condemning colonialism, 2131 (1965) on the Inadmissibility of Intervention in the Domestic Affairs of States and the Protection of Their Independence and Sovereignty, and finally 2625 (1970) on friendly relations.[7]

At this stage in history there was yet no self-styled international human rights movement in the world, and there barely was by the end of it. What is fascinating about these documents, instead, is that while fulsomely invoking human rights, they exacerbate the sovereigntist premises of national welfarism in view of memories of colonialism—including the colonialist entanglements of human rights in the 1940s. One can recall, after all, that Western policy as late as 1950 was not to arrest the minimal advance of international enforcement of human rights that a few advocates demanded, but to insert a colonial clause to ensure that human rights did not apply to imperial spaces. The new states pushed back in view of continuing empire—and apartheid (and later occupation). They invoked human rights to set up a shield against intervention, not as a rationale for it, except when ending colonialism was at stake. Just as with the Jews in the 1940s, the anticolonial response to

---

7. For further details, see my *Last Utopia*, Chapter 3, or "Imperialism, Self-Determination, and the Rise of Human Rights," in Iriye et al., eds., *Human Rights Revolution.*

atrocity was nationalism and sovereignty—not human rights in our contemporary sense.

Now for the third stage. Only at the dawn of the 1970s, and in particular after the Cold War, did a widespread humanitarian paradigm of human rights arise, to overtake and supersede the two earlier ones. It differed from the first paradigm in making atrocity-prevention, not welfare-promotion, the core of the human rights concept for a global or at least North Atlantic public. It differed from the second by blunting the extremism of anticolonial sovereigntism: a once colonial set of great powers was kept at bay by guaranteeing sovereign equality formally speaking, and insisting on insuperable barriers to intervention.

Why did this humanitarian paradigm arise? This question is as complicated as it is burning, but the most crucial fact is that its prestige coincided with the crisis of welfarism as an idealistic promise, as across the north Atlantic people replaced strong local solidarity with weak—and cheap—global solidarity, focused on what Didier Fassin calls "the condition of victimhood."[8]

If this is true, then the strenuous recent campaign to build a myth of what the 1940s clearly did not contribute, a global idealism of human rights like ours, has made recent commentators skirt the real significance of the period, not simply for observers at the time but most especially from a present-day perspective. After all, the prestige of human rights and the salience of human rights movements in our time have overlapped—in an

---

8. Didier Fassin and Richard Rechtman, *The Empire of Trauma: An Inquiry into the Condition of Victimhood*, translated by Rachel Gomme (Princeton, 2009); cf. Thomas Laqueur's review, "We Are All Victims Now," *London Review of Books*, July 8, 2010.

extremely eerie and disheartening coincidence—with the destruction since the 1970s of the grandiose dreams and partial realities that national welfarists introduced and achieved so prominently from the 1940s.

If it was not the Holocaust, meanwhile, that drove early understandings of human rights, Holocaust memory certainly did drive the last, humanitarian paradigm. And yet, what may have mattered most was the coincidence of that memory with the widespread perception, spoken loudly or kept close to the vest, that decolonization had gone dreadfully wrong. A recent scholar, Michael Rothberg, rightly emphasizes how German and colonial atrocity could be remembered together, but he might have gone even further—by acknowledging how crucial the memory of the Holocaust was to the origins of a human rights movement not so much outraged by imperial crime as it was depressed or angry about postcolonial failure.[9] Even as solidarity faltered as the best thing we can achieve, human rights became about atrocious cruelty as the worst thing we— or more accurately they—can do.

And yet there is no serious research on this conjuncture beyond the 1940s. At this stage of the scholarly conversation, having incorrectly framed the problem of how the Holocaust and human rights intersect as a story about the 1940s, no one has more than the faintest clue about how to solve it once the clock is properly set around the aftermath of decolonization. There are, it is true, very stimulating but generally unsatisfactory studies by sociologists like Jeffrey Alexander or Daniel Levy, whose empirically superficial abstractions do not fit with the details of what is already known, and so are

---

9. Michael Rothberg, *Multidirectional Memory: Remembering the Holocaust in the Age of Decolonization* (Stanford, 2009).

not very useful in framing new research agendas for historians.[10]

Consider two chronological boundaries. In the late 1960s, there was already a burgeoning invocation of genocide—against America in global protest of Vietnam, and in response to the Biafra crisis frequently framed as a genocide—but no clear connection yet between such mass atrocity and human rights as a concept. At least, very few observers invoked the latter in framing the former. By the early 1980s, for example in the campaigns to uncover the extent of the Cambodian genocide, the connection had been made.[11] The 1970s were the great age of the breakthrough of popular Holocaust memory— and the coincidence that human rights became such a popular lexicon then too ended up entangling them with each other in our moral imaginations. Of course, this generalization applies primarily to the north Atlantic, and historical research will have to consider how well it holds in other spaces (or whether it holds at all).

Once historians have worked out the belated relations of human rights and Holocaust memory in much more detail than they have so far, there will be a moral and

10. Jeffrey Alexander, *Remembering the Holocaust: A Debate* (New York, 2009); Daniel Levy and Natan Sznaider, *The Holocaust and Memory in a Global Age* (Philadelphia, 2005); Levy and Sznaider, *Human Rights and Memory* (State College, PA, 2010).

11. Compare on Vietnam, Samuel Moyn, "From Antiwar to Antitorture Politics," in Austin Sarat et al., eds, *Law and War* (Stanford, 2014); on Biafra, Lasse Heerten, "The Dystopia of Postcolonial Catastrophe: Self-Determination, the Biafran War of Secession, and 1970s Human Rights," in Jan Eckel and Samuel Moyn, eds, *The Breakthrough: Human Rights in the 1970s* (Philadelphia, 2014); and on Cambodia, Eva Marie Prag, "Becoming Conscious of the Killing Fields: American Representations of the Cambodian Genocide in the Age of Human Rights (1970–1990)," (MA thesis, Columbia University, 2013).

political balance sheet. For now, guessing what the bottom line will look like is all that seems possible. And there is clearly good on the positive side of the ledger. Self-evidently, atrocity prevention is a noble task. Defining a human rights agenda in its terms was not a negligible thing. It has provided a meaningful life for many people, whose activist and legal efforts deserve praise. And it has probably made a difference, if not in concrete cases of "intervention," then in educating the sensitivities of a world audience now far less complacent about horror.

And yet the confluence coincided with some losses. One of the worst outcomes of the imaginative linkage of the Holocaust and human rights is that it allows people to believe that the sole alternative to a humanitarian and human rights framework is genocidal violence or, at best, immoral complacency. Yet even when they are merely about resisting atrocity, human rights are a *reform project* in competition with other such projects. Some of these others—like nationalism and socialism—had to subside in their appeal to make way for human rights; others will simply fail to be invented so long as the intensive focus remains on preventing a *summum malum* rather than conceiving of a *summum bonum*. Put differently, the alternative to our contemporary humanitarian culture of human rights is not doing nothing. It is doing something else—and perhaps something better.

In this light, it is disturbing that the confluence of human rights and Holocaust memory came about as welfarism in its national, North Atlantic first version and in its more expansive anticolonial version were abandoned. A vision of global welfarism is a prospect that none of the three ages of human rights, and least of all the last one, has so far permitted. That hard truth is the obverse of the pre-eminence of human rights today.

7

TORTURE AND TABOO

We are disturbed about torture—yet again. What incest was for Oedipus and his Greek audience, torture is for us: the polluting stink that incites outrage and demands expiation. Even before its release in December, *Zero Dark Thirty*, Kathryn Bigelow's film about the hunt for Osama bin Laden after 9/11, was engulfed in a controversy over several scenes that seem to show that torture is effective. Three members of the Senate released a highly unusual statement, insisting that in its representation of torture, the film should have clearly condemned and rejected the practice. In a note to his staff, Michael Morell, the acting director of the Central Intelligence Agency, worried that the film suggested in too simplistic a way that torture was instrumental in locating the quarry. (He left open the question of whether torture ever works.)[1] On the News Desk blog of the *New Yorker*, Jane Mayer—whose investigative reporting for that magazine on the CIA's policy of extraordinary renditions, "black site" prisons and the brutal interrogation of terrorism suspects did so much to

---

[1]. Michael Morell, "Message from the Acting Director: 'Zero Dark Thirty,'" cia.gov/news.

spark the current debate on torture—took especially angry exception, writing that if Bigelow "were making a film about slavery in antebellum America, it seems, the story would focus on whether the cotton crops were successful." Mayer contends that *Zero Dark Thirty* not only falsifies history; it also disturbs a long-settled consensus that torture never produces useful intelligence and, for the sake of a Hollywood buck, risks a return to the ethically unthinkable. "Can torture really be turned into morally neutral entertainment?" Mayer asked. It was a rhetorical question.[2]

Torture is not just wrong or even criminal. It is taboo, a practice that marks the boundary between a community and what it treats as unconscionably reprobate or uncommonly terrifying. A taboo, wrote Sigmund Freud, glossing the Polynesian origins of the term, involves "holy dread" and "a sense of something unapproachable."[3] A taboo also reveals as much about those who enforce it as those who violate it, for a taboo reflects the overall value system that depends on its enforcement. But has torture, especially when practiced in defense of the nation, always seemed so scandalous?

As much as right-thinking journalists and politicians might like to presume otherwise, the question is far from rhetorical. Mayer argues that the problem with Bigelow's depiction of torture in *Zero Dark Thirty* "is not that it tells this difficult history but, rather, that it distorts it." Yet in her own justly celebrated journalism, unveiling the Bush administration's torture memos and honoring those who refused on principle to endorse such vile tactics, Mayer misrepresented a complicated history. Her work

2. Jane Mayer, "Zero Conscience in 'Zero Dark Thirty,'" *New Yorker* News Desk, December 14, 2012, newyorker.com/online/blogs.

3. Sigmund Freud, *Torture and Taboo*, translated by James Strachey (New York, 2001), pp. 21–2.

depends on the assumption that the taboo against torture
has been a stable norm for a very long time. No one had
ever done what John Yoo, author of several of the memos,
did when he worked for the Office of Legal Counsel in
the Bush White House, Mayer wrote. But was that
because the US government had never tortured before
and needed legal cover to do so for the first time? Or was
it because it had done so repeatedly, from the Philippines
to Vietnam, but had never needed to change the rules for
the sake of the job? Though it should provide Yoo no
comfort, the truth is that war crimes were far worse in the
American past, and his very acts suggested how novel and
powerful the taboo on torture had become. "This country has in the past faced other mortal enemies, equally if
not more threatening, without endangering its moral
authority," Mayer declared in the introduction to *The
Dark Side* (2008), a compilation of her classic pieces on
the use of torture during the "war on terror."[4] Who
exactly is distorting history?

The truth is that it took a very long time, morally speaking, for people here and abroad to mobilize against
torture.[5] Tobias Kelly's *This Side of Silence* calmly

4. Jane Mayer, *The Dark Side: The Inside Story of How the War
on Terror Turned into a War on American Ideals* (New York, 2008),
p. 9.

5. Compare Pierre Clastres, "Of Torture in Primitive Societies,"
in *Society against the State: Essays in Political Anthropology*, translated
by Robert Hurley (Cambridge, MA, 1987), along with more recent
postcolonial argument about radically different cultural regimes of pain:
Talal Asad, *Formations of the Secular: Christianity, Islam, Modernity*
(Stanford, 2003), Chapter 3, "Reflections on Cruelty and Torture";
and Veena Das, *Critical Events: An Anthropological Perspective on
Contemporary India* (Delhi, 1995), Chapter 7, "The Anthropology of
Pain." For interesting early modern speculation, see Lisa Silverman,
Tortured Subjects: Pain, Truth, and the Body in Early Modern France
(Chicago, 2001).

explains some of the factors underlying the shift in attitude that occurred a few decades ago.[6] A crucial date is 1973, when the non-governmental activists of Amnesty International, expanding their remit of challenging political imprisonment to include a campaign against torture, gave the norm a new global standing that continues to have wide resonance today. Using standard techniques of moral regulation—this time for the good—Amnesty succeeded in making the state's infliction of extreme physical pain anathema, though it was once a customary part of most cultures, an all-too-typical practice in the difficult search for truth and, in modern times, a surprisingly acceptable tool of governance, even in "enlightened" regimes.

Torture deployed for the sake of extracting evidence from witnesses became increasingly unacceptable after the Renaissance, and during the Enlightenment Voltaire and others assailed its use by the state.[7] Yet the distaste for torture was always intermittent, especially among citizens enjoined by their enlightened states to be decent at home, but who were willing to tolerate a different standard abroad, as well as during wartime. Torture was also banned in the written regulations around warfare between civilized states, which were sometimes taken to heart by the combatants—but the same was not true in colonial warfare, or in colonial rule.[8]

In 1948, torture was stigmatized by the Universal Declaration of Human Rights, when the memory of

---

6. Tobias Kelly, *This Side of Silence: Human Rights, Torture, and the Recognition of Cruelty* (Philadelphia, 2011).

7. See John Langbein, *Torture and the Law of Proof: Europe and England in the Ancien Régime* (Chicago, 1977); Lynn Hunt, *Inventing Human Rights: A History* (New York, 2007), Chapter 2.

8. See, e.g., R. W. Kostal, *A Jurisprudence of Power: Victorian Empire and the Rule of Law* (New York, 2008).

Nazi perfidy was still vivid. But as Kelly shows, the article on torture almost did not make it into the text, and torture remained widespread.[9] If a taboo emerged, it was only to the extent that most citizens of the Cold War era wanted to avert their gaze from torture rather than mobilize to stop it; and, as Darius Rejali suggested in *Torture and Democracy*, their governments entered a pact with them by keeping the violence secret and leaving no marks so as to keep it "clean."[10]

Against this background, Amnesty hewed out a new global consensus. Opening its campaign against torture with high-profile events on both sides of the Atlantic, it gathered thousands of signatures on its petitions. Soliciting the testimony of survivors, the group published reports on how torture remained a widespread and ingrained practice, lifting the cloak of secrecy and provoking government denials. Amnesty co-founder Seán MacBride won the Nobel Peace Prize in 1974 for the campaign, and the organization won its own Nobel three years later. All in all, it was one of the most successful exercises in moral consciousness-raising ever.

It occurred in connection with other causes. Decades after World War II, former democratic governments in places like Brazil, Greece and Chile fell to dictatorships, and reports of torture against political enemies soon followed. It was not so much that the use of torture was on the rise (though Amnesty insisted it was). Instead, it seemed as if the law of perpetual improvement were being glaringly violated, as countries with democratic traditions—even the birthplace of democracy itself—became the setting for this outmoded and barbaric practice. As Kelly reports, at just this moment British

---

9. Kelly, *This Side*, pp. 28–9.
10. Darius Rejali, *Torture and Democracy* (Princeton, 2007).

counterterrorism practices in Northern Ireland were also attracting novel scrutiny. British officials were irritated to discover that the interrogation techniques they had used in their policing and counterinsurgency operations in Palestine, Malaya, Kenya, Cyprus, Brunei, and Aden without a second thought—and without provoking any public scandal—were suddenly being greeted with outrage.[11]

In any event, by 1973 decolonization was largely over. Though, as Kelly says, the concern of Western citizens was primarily mobilized by instances of torture in Europe, or by its use against Latin Americans of European descent, they were now also less likely to avert their gaze from global violence or consider it part of the price of doing business. At this moment, their countries were either leaving their former colonies or had already gone. It may seem cynical to imply that it was this retreat from the violence of imperial rule that suddenly made torture beyond the pale for Westerners, especially if others were perpetrating it. But there is no other way to make sense of the timing of the norm's global emergence. The political theorist Judith Shklar responded to Amnesty's activism by calling physical cruelty "the worst thing we can do."[12] The truth seems to be that torture acquired its insidious glamour as the worst thing *they* do—once Western violence was done, and the places it had shaped for so long now looked like scenes of indigenous misrule.

As for Americans, in 1973 their government had just signed a peace treaty with Vietnam, which had important repercussions for the origins of human rights politics in the United States. (The historian Barbara

---

11. Kelly, *This Side*, pp. 6, 33.
12. Judith N. Shklar, *Ordinary Vices* (Cambridge, MA, 1984), p. 44.

Keys discusses this history in a brilliant and unsettling book, *Reclaiming American Virtue*.[13]) Revelations that torture was being perpetrated by a former client state made the most difference: the South Vietnamese kept political prisoners in the "tiger cages" of Côn Sơn Island until the glare of their exposure by the press grew too lurid (and the regime fell to communists). Amnesty's campaign eventually led to the UN's adoption of the Convention against Torture, which even the United States, forever bridling against potential infringements on its sovereignty, ratified in 1988.

These interacting causes instruct but also distract. Alone and together, they do not fully account for the singular horror of torture that has seized our moral attention, especially since 9/11 and the Abu Ghraib revelations. After all, our most recent controversy over torture involves our own state and how aggressive its military and civilian branches can be in their "war on terror." Establishing the continuity of present acts of torture with those from the past, as Laleh Khalili does in her startling book *Time in the Shadows*, is a pressing matter, but so too is tracing the emergence of the attitude that torture is a singular abomination and banning it our highest task.[14]

Behind all these factors for the shift in our contemporary moral consciousness lurks a deeper reason why torture has become a signature evil like no other. When evil threatens, taboos are respected rather than examined. In our own era, however, torture's incidence has been on the decline (the "war on terror" notwithstanding). And so it could be that our continuing preoccupation

13. Barbara J. Keys, *Reclaiming American Virtue: The Human Rights Revolution of the 1970s* (Cambridge, MA, 2014).

14. Laleh Khalili, *Time in the Shadows: Confinement in Counterinsurgencies* (Stanford, 2012).

with the subject is one more symptom of an exhausted political utopianism, a loss of faith in our ability to do more than keep evil—including our own—at bay.

In the summer of 1977, a young literary critic traveled to London to read Amnesty's accounts of torture. The book that emerged from the trip, *The Body in Pain*, made its author, Elaine Scarry, now a Harvard professor, our intellectual guide, and nearly thirty years on she remains a valuable proxy for our ethical perspective.[15] According to Scarry, "there may be no human event that is as without defense as torture."

In a certain way, Scarry's career has paralleled that of the taboo itself. When *The Body in Pain* appeared, accompanied by breathless endorsements from Susan Sontag and others and garnering stellar reviews in the national press, it instantly became a canonical book. Scarry, previously unknown, found herself immediately elevated to the empyrean for her moral intensity and weird charisma. If torture has become our execration, Scarry benefits from something like a sacred aura: that a few notable skeptics—such as Shklar and the philosopher Peter Singer—dared to call out her book for beginner's incompetence, unverifiable assertion and sheer charlatanry only helped to confirm her status.[16]

Scarry's writings are simply bizarre—albeit so strange as to disarm criticism. Her first book, like all her succeeding ones, requires the suspension of disbelief that intense visions always do, as Scarry goes her own way and asks you to follow her, with little rational justification, in

---

15. Elaine Scarry, *The Body in Pain: The Making and Unmaking of the World* (New York, 1985), especially pp. v, 326, 328, for evidence of the summer 1977 London trip to read Amnesty torture documents.

16. See Peter Singer, "Unspeakable Acts," *New York Review of Books*, February 27, 1986.

frequently bewildering directions. Opening with a meditation on Amnesty's torture reports, *The Body in Pain*
slowly and shockingly gives way to a homespun meta-
physics of demiurgic human creativity.

Pain, Scarry announces, is inexpressible. "English,"
she quotes Virginia Woolf as saying, "which can express
the thoughts of Hamlet and the tragedy of Lear, has no
words for the shiver or the headache."[17] The reason,
Scarry hypothesizes, is that pain, though it has a cause,
has no object; the eye sees something, the ear hears
something, the finger touches something, but the body
in anguish merely aches. In its most perfect epitome,
which is torture, the infliction of pain is an act of appro-
priation for the sake of empowerment. In torture,
language is used perversely to convert the victim's
torment into the interrogator's fraudulent mastery.
Torturers make use of the escalating pain they mete out
to build their—and their regimes'—immoral power.

Scarry did not dwell on torture exclusively; instead,
she made the body in pain—physical distress of any
sort—the foundation of human creativity. Everyone,
from the humblest artisan to the most gifted novelist,
creates in response to bodily suffering; unlike the appro-
priation enacted by torture, creation compensates or
substitutes for pain. Though torturers destroy or
"unmake" the world, pain serves constructively—in
texts ranging from the Bible to Karl Marx—as that
against which creation is asserted and conducted,
whether in the simplest tool or the grandest masterpiece.
The Bible, Scarry says, is a series of scenes of injuring,
but it underpins the imagination of God himself and the
new world he will bring about, while Marx rooted his
account of labor's creativity in physical suffering. The

---

17. Scarry, *Body in Pain*, p. 4.

pain of labor materializes in objects of creation. In this way, torture is the inverted likeness of the imagination; where the one destroys, the other fashions.

Scarry's brief inaugural meditation on "savage" torture, the most famous pages she has ever written, is a pivotal moment in our recent cultural history. Like a secular piece of scripture, *The Body in Pain*, published during the time when the Convention against Torture was moving from adoption by the United Nations to global ratification, made what would otherwise seem an inexplicable human evil the center of a vivid system of world-historical meaning. What also made the account famous was that it broke unceremoniously with the critical pieties of its day. Scarry was a new system-builder in an age of "postmodern" theory. Instead of treating the body as an amalgam of conflicting social codes, she insisted that it is a palpable, incontestable reality in response to whose suffering all of human culture is erected. As for the term "deconstruct," Scarry did use it—but not as the postmodernists did. For them, it named the practice of overturning oppositions in a discourse; for Scarry, it only referred to what torturers do in inflicting pain.

Further, Scarry's uncomplicated belief in the power of creation to change our lives and save—no, even make—the world seemed, for those who did not find it sophomoric, to be genial. Movingly defending beauty and treating it as a moral resource, Scarry broke with a critical culture of suspicion that unmasked art as ideology, instead offering a touchingly naïve appeal to the true, the good and the beautiful as if it were an act of unexampled sophistication. (Missing from her account of Marx is the critique of ideology, along with the class struggle and violent revolution.) And it worked, precisely because literary critics had followed fashion so far as to lose touch with what had always been the aesthetic basis of their role.

Even so, placing torture first, as Scarry did on the basis of her Amnesty documents, proved fateful. In the best meditation on Scarry's critical universe, fellow literary critic Geoffrey Galt Harpham observed that its "thickly affective atmosphere of intelligent compassion, of tender regard for the vulnerable human being," came linked, as if in reaction to the grisly particularities of torture, to "a committed moral optimism that was jarringly discordant with the witty and sophisticated disenchantment prevalent then and now."[18] Yet between the nether pole of torture and the high summit of creation, a crucial piece of terrain is missing in Scarry's thought: the place where the real politics of workaday institutions—the very ones that both cause torture and can avert it—happen. Indeed, how Scarry moved from an intense concern with torture to an aestheticism of creation seems as illustrative of a certain popular moral stance today as it is dubious. Beyond Amnesty's fact-finding, which she clearly prizes, Scarry speaks often of the need for political leaders to obey the law and for democracies to govern themselves. But when it comes to what the law should say, there are only vague statements. She focuses attention on a specific evil but leaves the good abstract.

Prescriptions are offered in *On Beauty and Being Just*, a fascinating essay in which Scarry proposes an ideal of symmetry in social relations that an attention to beauty might offer.[19] But perhaps because of her focus

---

18. Geoffrey Galt Harpham, "Elaine Scarry and the Dream of Pain," *Salmagundi*, no. 130/131 (Spring/Summer 2001): 206.
19. Scarry, *On Beauty and Being Just* (Princeton, 1999).

on bodies being tortured, bodies in pain—to which she can offer only the vague antidote of creation—the role of political institutions and the choice among them is left out. Though Judith Shklar organized her political theory around cruelty too, shortly before her death she indicted Scarry, in a withering review in the *London Review of Books*, for treating torture as a matter of "isolating individuals [who] do something in a vacuum."[20] Scarry has never seen torture (or creativity, for that matter) as a concrete social and political event linked to specific institutions.

In her scattered remarks on justice, Scarry interprets the politics of the social contract as a collective commitment not to injure. Though not fully wrong, this definition adheres to the most basic and limited purposes of collective political enterprise. In her polarized universe, in which ugly violence meets beautiful flowers, Scarry is Thomas Hobbes plus John Ruskin. The conjunction of pain and beauty leaves open all that humanity has learned, at least since Hobbes's pessimistic reaction to the English Civil War, about the possibility of solidarity in and through political fellowship, and the need to experiment with institutions to achieve it. To her credit, Scarry concluded *The Body in Pain* hopeful that it would "enable us to recognize more quickly what is happening not only in large-scale emergencies like torture or war but in other long-standing dilemmas, such as the inequity of material distribution."[21] But it is not surprising that her book has succeeded in focusing our taboos on one sort of thing rather than another.

---

20. Judith Shklar, "Torturers," *London Review of Books*, October 9, 1986.
21. Scarry, *Body in Pain*, p. 22.

In Harpham's estimation, Scarry, while utterly idio-syncratic, is also "a representative figure of the life of the mind in a time of trauma."[22]

Politics involves comparing always dirty regimes and seeking better alternatives, and the absence of this sphere is what is most questionable about Scarry's universe. That we focus on torture so single-mindedly—as if the institutional contexts for it and the institutional sequels to it were not more important—is due to historical experiences that, because they are the conditions of Scarry's criticism, may escape her gaze.

One influential public figure who found *The Body in Pain* compelling was the American philosopher Richard Rorty. As the repeated references to Scarry's "remarkable" inquiry in his landmark book *Contingency, Irony, and Solidarity* (1989) show, Rorty interpreted her argument to mean that torture is bad not so much because of the bodily pain it causes its victims, but instead because of the irremediable humiliation it forces on them. "The worst thing you can do to somebody," Rorty affirmed, "is not to make her scream in agony but to use that agony in such a way that even when the agony is over, she cannot reconstitute herself."[23]

In his own work, Rorty was primarily interested in figuring out what it would mean to leave the philosophical tradition behind, scrapping its search for some deep foundation that grounds all knowledge and ethics. But he was more concerned with the contingencies of private life as he struggled to preserve familiar liberal beliefs in personal freedom in the context of a moral

---

22. Harpham, "Elaine Scarry," p. 229.
23. Richard Rorty, *Contingency, Irony, and Solidarity* (Cambridge, 1989), pp. 36, 177.

theory lacking absolutes. He praised literary artists, together with the earlier philosophers he conscripted for his cause (from American pragmatists like John Dewey to European existentialists like Friedrich Nietzsche), to argue that there is no longer anything to govern our private self-creation—especially not a Platonic reality or higher authority to which creativity must conform. The goal of life for citizens of liberal democracies is to be personally interesting. In *The Body in Pain*, Scarry had not radically privatized the role of creativity; but Rorty did, relying on her account of torture to define the purpose of the public realm for his type of stay-at-home poet.

For Rorty, the highest—indeed, sole—goal of public institutions is to keep evil at bay for the sake of private self-creation. We should divide our libraries in two, he proposed: "books which help us become autonomous" and "books which help us become less cruel."[24] And torture, in Scarry's rendition, served him as the exemplar for how the politics of the public realm could go awry and infringe on private artistry by destroying self-creation. Strikingly, Rorty went so far as to redefine "solidarity" in terms of torture: solidarity is "the ability to see more and more traditional differences (of tribe, religion, race, customs, and the like) as unimportant when compared with similarities with respect to pain and humiliation."[25] Once we recognize that we are all potential victims of torture, in other words, we will

---

24. Ibid., p. 141. In a letter to the editor of the *Nation*, April 1, 2013, George Scialabba plausibly complained that Rorty centered his analysis around cruelty in general rather than torture in particular. But there is no gainsaying that Rorty's chapters in *Contingency*, which are his most theoretically rich account of politics, revolve around the example of torture as the epitome of cruelty in action.

25. Ibid., p. 192.

overcome our petty divisions for the sake of protecting our bodies from pain.

In two extraordinary (and extraordinarily flawed) chapters, Rorty turned to literature to illustrate the overwhelming political importance of cruelty and torture. He focuses on the last part of George Orwell's *1984*, in which the cunning Inner Party member O'Brien tortures the novel's hero, Winston Smith, to gain his compliance. Folded into Rorty's interpretation of the novel is an attack on the literary critic Raymond Williams, who had dismissed the last part of *1984* on the grounds that Orwell rejected torture so strenuously that he left politics behind.[26] Orwell's mistake, Williams insisted, was to make torture (and the power to humiliate in general) so crucial a concern; by doing so, Orwell tacitly assumed that power itself is evil and the best thing one could do was to avoid its workings, especially when it reached the extremity of torture. One could denounce torture, Williams countered, without ceasing to concern oneself with what sort of regime was perpetrating it and what sort of politics should replace it. To a Marxist like Williams, or a social democrat, or even a less reactive liberal, the limitation of Orwell's stance—indenturing the imagination to the specter of "endless torture," on the assumption that torture is the inescapable face of power—was its denial that power and imagination are necessary for creating a good regime.[27] Ultimately, what matters is the sort of social life that power and imagination can bring about, not just whether torture is averted.

Rorty, however, confined the imagination to the private sphere, restricting its use in public life to helping

26. Raymond Williams, *Orwell* (London, 1971).
27. Cited in Rorty, *Contingency*, p. 182.

one see how inimical to others cruelty can be. Torture became the new polestar of politics, Rorty insists, precisely because the dream of "a better world" which people had mobilized around and fought brutal hot and cold wars over in the twentieth century at some point stopped making sense. "We cannot tell ourselves a story about how to get from the actual present to such a future," he contends. "This inability to imagine how to get from here to there is a matter neither of loss of moral resolve nor of theoretical superficiality, self-deception, or self-betrayal. It is not something we can remedy . . . It is just the way things happen to have fallen out . . . This bad news remains the great intransigent fact of contemporary political speculation."[28]

Rorty's argument discloses some of the hidden assumptions of Scarry's position. Scarry never really defended the single-mindedness of making Amnesty's position on torture her polestar. Rorty did so for her— and us. The bad news of torture is very bad in a world where there is worse news: political hopelessness. For Rorty, idealism in public affairs is not possible in the foreseeable future, so our world of hierarchy and suffering just has to be accepted, with torture—which Orwell had shown insidiously at work even in the grandest efforts to remedy hierarchy and suffering—the only thing that you and I could possibly imagine fixing. True, Rorty was nominally a social democrat (as was Orwell), but placing torture first among public concerns belied this commitment. Torture matters greatly, Rorty writes, in "a globe divided into a rich, free, democratic, selfish, and greedy First World . . . and a starving, overpopulated, desperate Third World."[29] This state of affairs

28. Ibid., p. 182.
29. Ibid.

may not have been inevitable, but it is unalterable: "We liberals have no plausible large-scale scenario for changing that world."[30] But at least we can hate torture.

Leaving aside her quixotic attempt to trace the loss of TWA Flight 800 in 1996 to electromagnetic radiation, an undertaking she was allowed to pursue in three long articles published by the *New York Review of Books*, it was the hijacking and crashing of planes into the World Trade Center and the Pentagon, and the dishonorable acts committed during the two wars launched by the United States in their wake, that caused Scarry to move into political commentary in the last decade.[31] Yet her reasoning about torture after 9/11 has remained consistent with the pattern she laid down long before.

Scarry's first effort was characteristically unusual. Comparing the ways that two of the planes on 9/11 crashed, Scarry contends in *Who Defended the Country?* that United Flight 93, heading toward Washington, DC, but brought down by its passengers in a field in Pennsylvania, provided a generalizable example of how small, local groups are capable of defending themselves under their own power. It was true, of course, that American Flight 77, which hit the Pentagon, demonstrated the unpreparedness of the government and military for the events on that day. But it hardly follows that, as a general rule, ordinary citizens can and should take "injuring" into their own hands.[32]

The principle that Scarry champions—the democratic

---

30. Ibid.

31. Elaine Scarry, "The Fall of TWA Flight 800: The Possibility of Electromagnetic Interference," *New York Review of Books*, April 9, 1998.

32. Elaine Scarry et al., *Who Defended the Country?* (Boston, 2003).

control of self-defense—is laudable. In her published work (and presumably in her long-awaited *Thermonuclear Monarchy*), it informs her especially acerbic criticism of a nuclear weapons regime that operates entirely outside any popular control.[33] But her focus on excessive government, rampant technology and unchecked power leads her to embrace simple slogans like Democracy, Citizenship and Law. She never asks what kinds of democracy, citizenship and law are necessary to combat or contain the world's O'Briens and Strangeloves.

Similarly limited are the essays collected in *Rule of Law, Misrule of Men*.[34] Scarry responds indignantly to the frenzy of wrongdoing under George W. Bush, from the torture memos to executive overreach, but she directs her ire at the individuals breaking the laws and spends little time examining how much the laws already permitted them to do, and whether they could be changed. Indicting government lawlessness is appropriate and necessary, but aside from proceeding from a conventionally liberal view of what went wrong after 9/11, her essays fail to consider how much needs to be done politically after the torture has been stopped. Putting things generously, Richard Falk wrote in response to Scarry's post-9/11 writings that, "as with several other intriguing radicalisms, Scarry's argument recommends a return to a principled conservatism."[35] His point is that her nostalgia for self-government under law, though extremely basic and useful for various ends, could be a central progressive idea in a lawless age. But for Scarry herself, it

---

33. Elaine Scarry, *Thermonuclear Monarchy: Choosing Between Democracy and Doom* (New York, 2014).

34. Elaine Scarry, *Rule of Law, Misrule of Men* (Boston, 2010).

35. Richard Falk, "Too Utopian?" in *Who Defended the Country?* p. 37.

actually leads in the opposite direction: to a rather naïve commitment to the panacea of individual self-rule, including the notion that local control of violence is best (for Scarry, the Second Amendment protects this very value). Above all, Scarry's persistent appeal to the rule of law, as if it were the antidote to "injuring," ignores the degree to which existing laws permit and condone legitimate and even illegitimate violence. Aside from responding to the actions of a criminal administration, Scarry's critique of torture reflects a failure of constructive political imagination in a way that makes her a representative thinker of our time.

In the end, it does not appear Scarry ever considered the possibility that foregrounding the issue of torture so urgently could itself be a problem and not a solution. And in this way, too, she is emblematic. In her latest book, *Thinking in an Emergency*—published as the inaugural volume in the ambitious and interesting new Amnesty International Global Ethics Series, edited by Kwame Anthony Appiah—Scarry considers what sort of citizenship is possible for those confronted by evil.[36] In her newest post-9/11 criticism of government overreach, she describes what might happen if citizens simply refused to capitulate under pressure. For better and for worse, the exercise is vintage Scarry. Arresting in its prose, unexpected in its examples, and utterly personal in its arguments, *Thinking in an Emergency* is also bereft of any interest in the intermediate task of creating and comparing political alternatives.

As the book proceeds, Scarry insists on the importance of habit in sustaining citizen responses to destabilizing events (and the attempts by arrogant leaders to exploit

---

36. Elaine Scarry, *Thinking in an Emergency* (New York, 2011).

them for more power). Comparing citizenship to a series of activities, such as cardiopulmonary resuscitation, in which habit figures prominently—paramedics provide a proxy for the beating heart in order to help it resume its repetitious burden—Scarry recommends the force of tacit knowledge as the best defense against emergency. We should be like Benjamin Franklin, she says, who by creatively instilling routines in his day made himself a unique person.

The ability to think clearly in an emergency is, of course, critical, but so is the ability to think clearly beyond it. Yet, oddly, the theoretician of creativity neglects the fact that imagining and comparing the possible political worlds you and I might inhabit also makes creativity relevant to our collective lives. Tobias Kelly is right when he says that our current concern with torture does not rule out a richer engagement with some less reactive and more constructive political agenda. "The legal recognition of individual suffering may be just one goal among many, one way in which people may try to mobilize politically," he writes in *This Side of Silence*. "Wider ethical and political concerns can remain."[37] Yet this claim, while true in theory, has proven false in our practice: we have erected a taboo around torture even as our collective solidarity has faltered. These two events are not connected by necessity, but that does not mean they are easy to separate. At the very least, no one has figured out how to broaden the prohibition against the suffering caused by torture to include the suffering caused by a global inequality of wealth and power. Indeed, in some respects, we have achieved consensus denouncing the one only by averting our gaze from the other.

As a result of history and experience, we have gained

---

37. Kelly, *This Side of Silence*, p. 18.

the unprecedented ability to mobilize public opinion, nationally and globally, against leaders and regimes that take the low road, even as we've lost our collective ability to imagine any higher road for ourselves, whether in our own states or as a global community. Taboos empower, taboos paralyze. In a world where stopping torture should be a first step and not our only hope, we cannot be satisfied with a vision of creativity that is excessively abstract, entirely private and resolutely apolitical, any more than we can allow the worst that our governments have done to continue to distract us from the task of imagining and enacting the best we can make them do after the emergency is over.

8

SOFT SELLS: ON LIBERAL INTERNATIONALISM

A politics based on the rule of law and the rights of individuals at home has rarely translated into the same politics abroad. For a long time, liberal states were advocates not of global democracy promotion and "international human rights" so much as of a kinder, gentler empire. Back in the day, French reformers waxed poetic about how "colonial humanism" would realize the civilizing mission their empire had long promised the natives. At the turn of the twentieth century, Lord Cromer, the consul-general of Britain in Egypt, defended the British Empire by denouncing other empires from Rome forward. In them, he explained, "the subject was regarded as existing for the empire rather than the empire for the subject." For Lord Cromer, Britain's global ascendancy fell into a different category, because it promoted "the moral and material elevation" of "the subject races which were brought under her sway." Compared with prior and rival empires, Britain provided the right sort of domination—and only "an extreme radical visionary" could make the mistake of supposing that the world would be better off without it.[1]

Such soft sells of hard power are reminders that, free trade aside, a domestic commitment to liberal values had very little impact on the chilling and sometimes violent quest for wealth, security and order that modern European states conducted beyond their borders. But how different is the United States, with its proud traditions of constitutional government and fundamental rights? For a moment in the 1990s, it looked as if the American school of thought known as "liberal internationalism" was close to realizing its fondest dreams. The global order it envisioned—and which it claimed had already materialized to a striking degree—would provide the benefits not only of nineteenth-century free markets but also of twentieth-century human rights. As a leading liberal internationalist, G. John Ikenberry, writes in *Liberal Leviathan*, for more than four decades the United States had cultivated this post-imperial world, crafting—and, when necessary, submitting to—its multilateral rules and acting as the linchpin of its mostly consensual security arrangements.[2]

But even liberal internationalists, like Cromer earlier, cannot imagine a world beyond domination. Ikenberry contends that when the United States had the torch passed to it by Britain as the new liberal standard-bearer during World War II, it decisively moved liberal internationalism away from imperialism toward a new and benevolent kind of hegemonic leadership. Power now served morality, with the international community standing ready to

---

1. Citations in Robert L. Tignor, "Lord Cromer: Philosopher and Practitioner of Imperialism," *Journal of British Studies* 2, no. 2 (May 1963): 145, 147.

2. G. John Ikenberry, *Liberal Leviathan: The Origins, Crisis, and Transformation of the American World Order* (Princeton, 2011).

right wrongs whenever the spontaneous workings of the global system were threatened. Claiming they were the most recent inheritors of this old vision, and seeing themselves in the vanguard of history, liberal internationalists explained after the fall of the Soviet Union how long-dormant plans were finally coming to fruition in a world order that, under America's watch, was enjoying unparalleled freedom and prosperity.

The dawn of a long day turned out to be the dusk of a short one. After 9/11, George W. Bush quickly and unceremoniously upended a state of affairs that, according to Ikenberry's scholarship, Americans had spent decades reinforcing. Bush trashed multilateralism in foreign affairs, insisting that America had to "go it alone" when terrorism threatened; as a result, he treated global institutions that the United States had had a hand in creating as irritating obstacles to sovereignty—if they were not simply irrelevant. Counting himself among liberals offended by Bush, Ikenberry writes that the president "presented an extraordinary puzzle."[3] Adding insult to injury, the Great Recession that followed the political disarray of the Bush years has shaken the material foundations of American leadership and, in turn, the liberal order American internationalists have envisioned.

Ikenberry's attempt to reclaim liberal internationalism for the future is nothing if not courageous, because the chances of success seem slight. What seems incredible about this hulking leviathan now is not its beneficence abroad as much as its sclerosis at home. Even so, Ikenberry boldly concludes that the sorrows of liberal internationalism are temporary, and that sunny optimism about the long run is justified.

---

3. Ibid., p. xiii.

Unfortunately, aside from offering a psychological tonic, *Liberal Leviathan* does not give grounds enough for a confident bet on this faltering colossus—except perhaps the other way.

A professor at Princeton University, Ikenberry is perhaps the most acute member of the club of liberal internationalists gathered there. Like Woodrow Wilson, their honorary predecessor from the sleepy New Jersey town, liberal internationalists provide theoretical rationales for the American policy shop that they sometimes directly serve. Ikenberry has worked for the State Department's Policy Planning Staff, founded in 1947, and his close colleague Anne-Marie Slaughter recently directed it for a spell.

Several years ago, with the acrid smell of war in the air, charges of American imperialism were ubiquitous. For Ikenberry, it remains terribly important to defend America from accusations of empire. He starts out with abstract theory. Once a state is in the ascendant, it can impose its will on others by force or by consent. But whereas an imperial state is the powerful hub of a spoked wheel, a hegemon like the United States will construct a rule-based order and entice others to voluntarily join a multilateral web. Unlike an empire, which acts unilaterally and unpredictably, a hegemon creates legitimacy by propounding rules for states to which it also submits.

The trouble with these arguments is that Ikenberry does not establish a bright line between empire and hegemon. He is aware that, since the publication of John Gallagher's and Ronald Robinson's famous essay, historians of the nineteenth century have argued that the British state came to work through "informal empire," with the construction of a free-trade order as its aim and the use of military force and even direct administrative presence as the last resort rather than the first choice to enforce that order.[4] Other historians have since emphasized that, especially in the later nineteenth century, the British Empire also made a decisive move to "indirect" rule through local elites—an arrangement, Ikenberry acknowledges, that hegemony also relies on, such as when under decolonization sovereignty passed to new states. Empire in its informal and indirect character could verge on hegemony.

Correspondingly, hegemony is on a continuum with empire. "Weaker and secondary states are formally sovereign and the extent and mechanisms of domination will tend to be looser and less formal," Ikenberry says of hegemonic arrangements.[5] But sometimes empire is already domination in kinder and gentler form. Nothing of much consequence hangs on isolating the point at which empire ends and hegemony begins, because "looser and less formal" domination cuts across the divide between them. The attempt to justify that dominance in the highest moral terms does so too, as Lord Cromer's words about the British Empire attest. As a result, if there is no point to unmasking the hegemonic United States as an empire, there is also no obvious reason to argue, as Ikenberry does, that its mode of hegemony is "profoundly distinctive" from empire either.[6]

It seems obvious that a hegemon can never break cleanly from the imperial hub-and-spokes model in the

---

4. John Gallagher and Ronald Robinson, "The Imperialism of Free Trade," *Economic History Review*, new series 6, no. 1 (1953): 1–15; see also Wm. Roger Louis, ed., *Imperialism: The Robinson and Gallagher Controversy* (New York, 1976).

5. Ikenberry, *Liberal Leviathan*, p. 70.

6. Ibid., p. 61.

name of multilateralism and what Ikenberry calls "leading through rules." To the extent it wants to exercise greater power, it will never allow negotiations to happen among equals, even in the international institutions it may have helped to establish, without exerting back-channel pressure to guide negotiations to the desired result. And it always maintains the right to walk away from the negotiating table and scramble the fighter jets when "negotiation" leads to an unacceptable outcome. Ikenberry insists that only empire relies on force, "at least in the last instance."[7] But the same is true of hegemony. Empire bleeds into hegemony because hegemony sometimes bleeds.

Continuing his theorizing, Ikenberry intensively examines liberal versions of hegemony, which he says boil down to domination based on multilateralism and negotiated consent rooted in universal values, rather than imposed arrangements and self-dealing backed up by violence. But because the divide between empire based on power and hegemony based on consent is muddy, liberalizing forms of empire have existed, to which hegemony could simply add more liberalism. At best, Ikenberry can argue only that hegemony can become relatively, not absolutely, liberal. He concedes as much when he writes charmingly throughout the book that American hegemony has had "liberal characteristics."[8] This is like saying that a poor man has "wealthy characteristics" because he is wearing a clean shirt, and very different from saying he is rich.

Most troubling, Ikenberry treats liberalism and hegemony as consistent, even though they are in deep

---

7. Ibid., p. 73.
8. Ibid., pp. 22, 25, 122, 254, 334.

tension. For if an international order becomes more liberal, it must become less hegemonic. Ikenberry's ideal of liberal hegemony suggests that to the extent the leading nation in the system bases its rule on high principle rather than open selfishness, it will gain more legitimacy as subordinate states believe the hype. Yet it also follows that a liberal hegemony will have to take seriously its commitment to the real, rather than merely formal, sovereignty of the state players.

The fraught tensions in the model of liberal hegemony, not its world-historical breakthrough, may be what's most distinctive about it. While guarding against conservatives to his right, Ikenberry equally avoids the extreme, radical or visionary hope to his left of a world beyond domination. He does not say that the egalitarian moral principles of justice championed by liberalism make the hierarchy of wealth and power upon which the system is based seem the height of unfairness. Only in a footnote does he make an observation that threatens to undermine the entire book: "Hegemony may be put at the service of creating an open and rule-based order, but hegemony is itself not democratic."[9] It is not liberal either.

Ikenberry is not wrong to argue that hegemony can become more liberal. Yet he never shows how a hegemonic order could become generally, mostly or completely liberal. Ikenberry is not really entitled to say, even on theoretical grounds, that any hegemony could ever qualify as fully consistent with liberal values. Certainly America's hegemony after World War II never did.

It is not just the abstract possibility of liberal hegemony that matters to Ikenberry. He tries to prove that

---

9. Ibid., p. 299.

American hegemony in practice fits the theoretical model. However, the history he tells inadvertently suggests that liberal internationalism must be a lot younger than he claims.

Ikenberry's history of American liberal internationalism begins with Woodrow Wilson. After Iraq, Ikenberry, Slaughter and others gathered in Princeton to refute worrisome charges, both academic and popular, that Bush was not the betrayal of "Wilsonianism" but its culmination. The debate was later published as a book called *The Crisis of American Foreign Policy*.[10] But everybody in the room agreed that Wilsonianism represented a single, continuous tradition. It is true that Wilson had an internationalist vision and was a liberal. However, the version of internationalism he backed is rather different from the one endorsed by today's liberal school. His famous Fourteen Points, devised to guide the construction of global order after World War I, emphasized peaceful coexistence under free trade. They offered national self-determination to some peoples living under the empires on the losing side, but said nothing about democratic government or human rights.

After 1945, in Ikenberry's telling, Americans led by forming a liberal system in which their power worked in part through the promotion of liberal values like human rights. Ikenberry frequently refers to a "human rights revolution" that was "deeply rooted in a progressive liberal vision that emerged in the 1940s."[11] But FDR's influence on international human rights in the '40s was not rooted in a terribly progressive vision and did not foster a revolution. Throughout the war FDR dreamed

---

10. G. John Ikenberry et al., *The Crisis of American Foreign Policy: Wilsonianism in the Twenty-First Century* (Princeton, 2008).

11. Ikenberry, *Liberal Leviathan*, p. 191 as well as pp. 246–7, 276, 296, 302.

of dividing the globe into zones of influence policed by superpowers, and he consented to a world organization on the condition that superpowers could achieve balance through it, an arrangement that eventually came to pass with the creation of the UN Security Council. His successor, Harry Truman, moved America into a Cold War that was not much about leading through rules or promoting human rights.

This was hegemony, yet it was hardly liberal. Strangely, though half his book is supposed to illustrate his theory of liberal hegemony since 1945, Ikenberry does not talk much about the Cold War, the largest component of the era by far. He acknowledges that liberal internationalism of the form he favors was "less obvious" throughout the period, given the pre-eminence of Cold War imperatives, yet he excludes the Cold War from his book as an apparently unrelated sideshow.[12] Ikenberry does admit that his thesis about the post–World War II American construction of a liberal international order works solely for Western Europe (and Japan), but he omits a lot even there. In places like Greece and Portugal, American hegemony worked through tools like proxy warfare and friendly dictators—and did not seem very liberal at the time. And then there are the parts of the globe that liberalism did not reach. "Triumphs and setbacks followed," he summarizes.[13] But "setback" is hardly an honest way to characterize events, like the Vietnam War, otherwise omitted from your story.

It was only after Vietnam—beginning in a moment of guilt and introspection and continuing in a post–Cold War mood of optimism and power—that liberal internationalism assumed its current form, stressing rules and

12. Ibid., p. 168.
13. Ibid., p. 62.

rights. Intellectually, liberal internationalism is really a
product of the 1970s and '80s, an era in which what it
meant to be a liberal in foreign affairs pivoted in the aftermath of catastrophe. Revealingly, surveys of usage show
that the phrase "liberal internationalism" circulated
widely only after 1980. (For anyone curious, "hegemony" is much older, as its Ancient Greek roots suggest. In
the twentieth century, the term was mainly associated
with Antonio Gramsci's anatomy of bourgeois rule
through consent; it was also used by certain Nazi theore-
ticians to define the global order they were planning.
Only much later did liberal political scientists begin to use
it as a term of praise for American dominance.[14])

The liberal internationalist's account runs roughshod
over the American past, and disguises the intellectual
origins of his own position. When it came into its own
in the 1990s, liberal internationalism suppressed its
complicated history, and Ikenberry's rather romanti-
cized version is a good example. Backdating its origins
provides it with the distinction of a tradition, but it also
conceals a lot of evidence about alternative projects
undertaken along the way. Just as liberalism had once
typically meant support for imperialism in the nineteenth century, its American forms after World War II
favored fierce and direct Cold War engagement alongside containment, as the history of the Vietnam era
shows most graphically.

How, then, can the liberal internationalist bring a
sunny perspective to a messy record? The liberal internationalist might acknowledge that "mistakes were made,"

14. Heinrich Triepel, *Die Hegemonie: Ein Buch von führenden
Staaten* (Stuttgart, 1938); Carl Schmitt, "Führung und Hegemonie,"
Schmollers Jahrbuch 63 (1939): 513–20, reprinted in Schmitt, *Staat,
Großraum, Nomos: Arbeiten aus den Jahren 1916–1969*, ed. Günter
Maschke (Berlin, 1995).

and that (just as in the earlier British case) American liberalism moved in the direction of rules and rights only after other methods proved counterproductive—and, ultimately, once the Soviet threat was put down by any means necessary. But Ikenberry does not proceed this way. He prefers to bury the mixed bag of the past, or to cloak its less uplifting contents in euphemisms. Such a history of American ascendancy seems primarily directed to Americans without much of a memory. Its chief function is public relations, the promotion of optimism about the present and future. But just because fairy tales soothe anxieties does not mean they are true.

Though he clearly began this book in order to defend America from charges of empire and to show the Bush era to be an accidental and temporary divergence from America's beneficent mission, Ikenberry just as clearly completed it as the financial crash revealed a different set of problems. If Bush forced liberal internationalists like Ikenberry to insist that the uses of America's dominance are different from its abuses, the crash prompted fears that its dominance is not long for this world.

The subtlest chapter of Ikenberry's book shows the alternative paths faced by a hegemon when it becomes uniquely powerful in a unipolar world, as was the case for the United States after 1989. It is a rich and rigorous survey of different possible outcomes. Ikenberry judiciously explains how unopposed power could entice the United States into an imperial trajectory, even as the forces of kind-hearted sympathy incite "crosscutting incentives" to make the country's dominance consensual and even charitable.[15]

But one of the most repeated and interesting reasons

---

15. Ikenberry, *Liberal Leviathan*, Chapter 4, p. 142.

Ikenberry offers for the United States to stay true to a liberal course is that liberal internationalism offers the best possible future for a unipolar power confronting its inevitable decline. The point of setting up an international system based on rules and rights, Ikenberry frequently if quietly notes, is never just to win consent now; it is also to entrench or lock in arrangements that favor a hegemony that cannot last. "If the rules and institutions are deeply embedded in wider systems of politics and economics, the order itself is made more durable and can last even into the future when the power of the hegemonic state declines," he observes.[16]

Such passages are indicative of the current state of liberal internationalism, which has moved on from its post-1989 position that liberalism and hegemony coincide or even depend on each other. Its new agenda is to figure out how to encode its values on the world order before the arrival of what Fareed Zakaria has called the "post-American" era.[17] These days, the high-minded statements of the spokesmen of liberal internationalism may reflect fear more than hope. It is easy to see, after all, that when its ability to set the agenda of the world order is on the wane, a great power will fret about its values more than ever.

Ikenberry concludes by suggesting how important it is that liberal values prosper in a world where American ascendancy is qualified or undone—and they can

---

16. Ibid., p. 181. Jenny Martinez draws a similar conclusion explicitly from her study of the slave trade: "At a time when US military and economic power is at a peak . . . the United States should consider projecting that power onto the future by creating and supporting stable international legal institutions rather than fostering a world order based on power alone." Jenny S. Martinez, *The Slave Trade and the Origins of International Human Rights Law* (New York, 2012), p. 171.

17. Fareed Zakaria, *The Post-American World* (New York, 2008).

prosper only if Barack Obama and his heirs make good on their passing chance to augment the liberalism of the world order. Yet it seems implausible that a new era of multipolarity or outright Chinese hegemony will especially favor the values Americans learned to champion only yesterday.

In a late section of his book, Ikenberry speculates that China's rise, if current trends continue, need not overturn the liberal order America has often promoted abroad as a general policy, especially under recent Democratic presidents. That order is so good, Ikenberry suggests, that China could and probably should try to join it rather than beat it. Here Ikenberry's moralism may interfere with his realism. That for the first twenty years of its existence China's communist government was excluded from the United Nations, which Ikenberry portrays as a manifestation of America's liberal internationalism, may lead China to wonder if other plans are in order.

What Ikenberry calls admiringly the "liberal Leviathan" of America's beneficent power could soon be a beached whale on the shore of an unknown future. Neither Ikenberry nor anyone else can predict what will happen. In the meantime, only one thing seems certain. Whoever seizes hegemony in an era of American decline will inevitably follow America's recent liberal internationalists in offering versions of history suggesting the moral propriety of their own inheritance of the globe. And they will have their own policy intellectuals struggling to prove that their dominance really is the best thing for a world that suspects otherwise.

EPILOGUE:
THE FUTURE OF HUMAN RIGHTS

To know what to make of human rights in the future, the first step is to understand what they have made us. They allowed us to adopt a utopian stance to the world. But this turn to utopia did not begin from scratch. It happened only after other, perhaps more inspiring utopias failed.

It seems odd to say that the utopian imagination has to start from the real world. But when it comes to international human rights, it is clear that utopia and reality do not so much exclude as depend on each other. At least, the hope embodied in human rights norms and movements, which germinated in the last part of the twentieth century, emerged from a realistic assessment of what sort of utopianism might make a difference.

One response to this discovery, it seems, is a proposal to return to the utopian imagination in its pure form, divorced from attempts to institutionalize it. When Plato earned Niccolò Machiavelli's scorn for dreaming of a politics based on a different sort of men than in fact existed, perhaps the Florentine neglected the value of thought experiments even if they prove entirely useless.[1] If the utopia of human rights emerged out of a historic compromise with reality, then perhaps the very attempt at compromise was a mistake: a better utopianism would proceed from the refusal to pay reality the respect of conforming to it.

I think this stance is wrong. Human rights at least answered to the need to begin utopia from the way things are now. Instead, my worry is that human rights have conformed *too much* to reality. The utopian challenge presented by human rights has proved so minimal that they easily became neutered, and were even invoked as excuses—for example, in wars serving other interests—for choices their original advocates did not intend.

Let me explain how I think international human rights became our current utopia and how they need to better resist the world they have so far failed to transform. To do so, they should work on the basis of the way the world is, and they should find a better compromise between utopianism and realism than has thus far been realized.

I have long been fascinated by understanding the hold of international human rights on the utopian imagination since these norms—together with the advocacy and mobilization that surround them—have become so appealing and prestigious in today's developed world. Taking up the question of when precisely a concept so central to the moral consciousness of so many idealists today became the supreme cause, I offer an unexpected answer: human rights as we understand them were born yesterday. Human rights

---

1. See David M. Estlund, *Democratic Authority: A Philosophical Framework* (Princeton, 2008), Chapter 14, "Utopophobia: Concession and Aspiration in Democratic Theory."

crystallized in the moral consciousness of people only in the 1970s, whether in Europe, Latin America, or the United States, and in transnational alliances among them.

To make this argument plausible required looking back at prior meanings of rights claims, which certainly were made—but which generally worked very differently. It was also crucial to carefully examine eras in which the notion could have spread in a broad-based movement, and could have become a touchstone, but failed to do so: notably the aftermath of World War II, when many people dreamed of a new deal, and during the decolonization that followed almost immediately. Finally, it was of great importance to analyze international lawyers more specifically, to ask when they became so closely identified with human rights politics even though they were peripheral to most of the uplifting movements in modern history; my answer is that it was around the same time as everybody else.

There were many reasons this happened. The chief one is a widespread disappointment with earlier, hitherto more inspirational forms of idealism that were failing. Human rights took their place. Human rights emerged as the last utopia.

Surveying both the scholarly and popular attention to the history of human rights, I found a shocking mismatch between common attempts to attribute the concept to the Greeks or the Jews, early modern natural law thinkers or French revolutionaries, and the far more recent conjuncture which my evidence suggested. (One book even went back to the Stone Age![2]) Now it is true that many historical ideologies across the millennia make

2. Micheline R. Ishay, *The History of Human Rights: From Ancient Times to the Globalization Era* (Berkeley, 2004).

morality and humanity central. But they do so in starkly different ways than in human rights movements today. Even as late as the revolutionary era of European and American history, after which "the rights of man" became a watchword, it was universally assumed that the goal was that a state—even a nation-state—would protect them.

Then there were fights within these states to define the entitlement of membership. For this reason, if one likes, there was a "rights of man" movement before there was a human rights movement, and it was called nationalism. Yet human rights today are neither revolutionary in their associations nor offer entitlements based on common membership in a space of protection, whether within or beyond the nation-state. And while it is true that a critique of national "sovereignty" bloomed before, during, and after World War II, when the Universal Declaration of Human Rights (1948) was framed, I also found the extraordinary attention this era gets among scholars and pundits to be misplaced. It is not even clear how many people who talked of human rights in the 1940s had in mind the creation of supranational sorts of authority on which "human rights" are now based. In any case, almost no one appealed to human rights then, either in an old or new version.

Far more significant was that human rights were introduced in the midst of World War II as a replacement for the liberation from empire of which most around the world dreamed—as a kind of consolation prize, that was therefore spurned. At the end of the conflict, much of the world remained colonized, but many took empire to be at an end. Yet not only did human rights not imply the end of empire (indeed the imperial powers were their most significant proponents);

many thought the Allies in their Atlantic Charter had promised decolonization, then took that promise back even as talk about "human rights" began.

Meanwhile, in the north Atlantic world, contests over a fraying wartime welfarist consensus took pride of place. The pressing problem as most people understood it was not how to move beyond the state, but what sort of new state to create. And in this situation the fiction of a moral consensus of "human rights" provided no help. Instead, everyone accepted the political battle.

Ironically, in the 1970s, the very moralistic consensus that once provided no help offered salvation. With the exhaustion of reform schemes in the East behind the Iron Curtain, and in the West with the collapse of student dissent, it did not seem feasible to dream of a better world the old way: by proposing a genuine and controversial political alternative.

In the East, dissidents recognized that such programs would be crushed. A morality of human rights provided an "anti-politics" to resist and indict the communist state. In the West, a moral alternative beckoned too—especially for idealists who had tried other things first and found them equally wanting. It also made sense in an America seeking recovery from the self-imposed disaster of Vietnam. For a brief moment, and to liberals most of all, American president Jimmy Carter's moralistic criticism of politics—as he chastised his country in terms of sin for its Vietnamese catastrophe—resonated with voters.

In view of the historical claims, some foundations for political argument now seem stronger than before, and others weaker. Clearly, thinking that international human rights have been God-given or naturally occurring, or even that they were a legacy of continuous moral insight following the genocidal horror of World War II, is mistaken.

Human rights came to make sense in a world of decolonized states (but in which not all states are trust-worthy.) Outrages against humanity like the slave trade once justified empire, as in the "scramble for Africa" after 1885; now they justify opprobrium against states that spent the first decades after World War II winning independence from empire. And even for Westerners—especially for Westerners—human rights were discovered by masses of people only after they had first tried other things, and given up on them in despair. Our idealism is one born of disappointment, not of horror or of hope.

But this suggestion does not translate easily into a set of specific consequences. If I am right, even when it comes to some of the beliefs people cherish most, history shows that they are always up for grabs. They may settle for a while, but even then are never stable. And this also means the burden falls on the present not to turn to the past for reassurance, but to decide for itself what to believe and in what way to change the world. History at its best liberates, but does not construct. Yet perhaps it offers a lesson all the same about what sort of idealism people should, or at least can, seek.

For the longest time in modern history, programs for bettering the world mattered most when they were politically controversial—such as when they sought to overturn the status quo. The achievement of the nation-state required dispensing with kings and aris-tocrats, just as the "rights of man movement" of the decolonized twentieth century demanded that empires should finally end. In the 1940s, human rights were bypassed because they offered the mere fiction of a moral consensus that plainly did not match the need for political choice.

The 1970s began an exceptional period in which the morality of human rights made sense; if and when that period ends, the need for contestatory political options may once again seem the most relevant one to meet. Of course, every or almost every political agenda appeals to transcendent moral norms. But programmatic politics is never about those moral norms alone. It assumes that the other side—for politics always has at least two sides—can likewise appeal to moral norms. So politics becomes a battle, hopefully waged through persuasive means from advertising to arguments, to gain power and enact programs.

Strangely, it is still a taboo to think this is also what should occur in international affairs. Partisanship acceptable at home—the ordinary contest for power amongst parties—is not openly available abroad, except through the alliance or contention of states alone rather than of broader parties or movements. Instead, thanks in large part to human rights, agendas for the world are argued in terms of morality.

For contemporary international human rights, there is only one side. The invasion of some country is demanded as following from the moral norm of the responsibility to protect, while a philosopher burning with shame at the poverty of the globe insists that morality requires economic redistribution. Humanitarian militarism is not defended as a highly political calculus, while the moral principle demanding redistribution does not by itself tell us how to realize it—though it will necessarily involve a potentially violent agenda of taking wealth from the powerful and giving it to the wretched of the earth.

Of course, the struggle for power is equally operative

at the global level. But because no one has discovered a way to constrain partisanship in international affairs—which has so frequently led to military hostilities—it has seemed preferable to argue in absolute or sentimental moral terms. The response to this worry about "politicizing" world affairs is that the global space is already a realm of power politics. Because of this reality, invoking moral principles will either have no effect, like the philosopher's complaint about poverty, or will mask the realities of power, as when humanitarian invasions occur. Pretending everyone already agrees with invoked moral norms does not change the fact that nobody does, or that people interpret them under the pressures of interest and partisanship.

The conclusion is that we can and should risk the development of more openly partisan enterprises in international affairs. The choice is not between whether to have them or not, but whether they are explicit or not. Another way to put this claim is in terms of Friedrich Engels's old contrast between utopian socialism and scientific socialism. His distinction was confused—if Marxist socialism was anything, it was utopian. But Engels was right to draw a distinction between utopias that acknowledge that they are controversial and oppositional, and therefore need to descend into the programmatic contest for power, and those that pretend that wishful thinking alone will change the world. The former approach needs to be recovered for utopia's sake, because the latter constantly proves ineffectual. "Human rights," in short, need to become more scientific.

It is here that the puzzle of contemporary human rights as a set of global moral principles and sentiments becomes clearest. As generally presented, they do not intervene in power politics. But just for that reason, they seem often to make little practical difference, amounting to an ornament on a tragic world which they do not transform. Because they are not realistic enough, they end up accommodating reality too much. A better compromise between utopianism and realism is required. How to find this compromise is anything but obvious. But it may help to conclude with a list of theses that indicate the sort of compromise I have in mind.

A politics of human rights must involve a transformation in steps. Radical politics have long been torn between the options of reform and revolution; but if anything has been learned on the left, it is the need to reject this dichotomy. Instead, the goal should be to take international human rights ideas and movements as they are, and radicalize them from there.

A politics of human rights must acknowledge that it is mobilizational. No casebook of international human rights law contains a section on human rights as a global movement. Instead, human rights norms are presented as norms to be enforced by judges. Realists know this presentation is not only historically false; it also avoids scrutiny of the conditions in which movements succeed.[3] For the sake of the non-partisanship that judging seems to demand, the role of contemporary judges depends on suppression of the fact that they are in league with a global movement of opinion. An occasional judge, like Antônio Augusto Cançado Trindade (who sits on the International Court of Justice), is more honest about his desire to affiliate with "humanity" as

3. For more insistence in this direction, see my "Do Human Rights Treaties Make Enough of a Difference?" in Costas Douzinas and Conor Gearty, eds., *Cambridge Companion to Human Rights Law* (Cambridge, 2012).

the source of human rights law.[4] But the moment judges are recognized as mobilizational agents, hard questions about whether they are the right agents start to be posed.

A politics of human rights must transcend judges. History shows that movements relying on judges alone are weak. In American history, judges succeeded in forcing genuine political change in the name of moral norms only when they allied with grassroots political movements. As the grassroots lost strength, judges did too. In any case, judges today have power to mobilize for human rights only in highly specific institutional contexts: in domestic polities that give them a role, or regional courts gathering together nations that have

---

4. Consider this remarkable language from an advisory opinion when he sat on the Inter-American Court of Human Rights: "It is not the function of the jurist simply to take note of what the States do, particularly the most powerful ones, which do not hesitate to seek formulas to impose their 'will' ... [The law] does not emanate from the inscrutable 'will' of the States, but rather from human conscience. General or customary international law emanates not so much from the practice of States (not devoid of ambiguities and contradictions), but rather from the *opinio juris communis* of all the subjects of International Law (the States, the international organizations, and the human beings). Above the will is the conscience ... Law is being ostensibly and flagrantly violated, from day to day, to the detriment of millions of human beings, among whom [number] undocumented migrants all over the world. In reacting against these generalized violations of the rights of undocumented migrants, which affront the juridical conscience of humankind, the present Advisory Opinion of the Inter-American Court contributes to the current process of the necessary *humanization* of International Law ... In so doing, the Inter-American Court bears in mind the universality and unity of the human kind, which inspired, more than four and a half centuries ago, the historical process of formation of the *droit des gens*. In rescuing, in the present Advisory Opinion, the universalist vision which marked the origins of the best doctrine of International Law, the Inter-American Court contributes to the construction of the new *jus gentium* of the XXIst century." Inter-American Court of Human Rights, Advisory Opinion OC-18/03 (September 17, 2003), on the Juridical Condition and Rights of Undocumented Migrants.

already agreed to cede some sovereign prerogatives to judicial elites. For human rights to make more of a difference, the movement has to be more honest about the fact that its success depends on its own mobilizational strength and grassroots penetration. For this reason, Amnesty International's recent decision to return to its mobilizational roots and cultivate local centers of authority is a promising step in the right direction. But few other NGOs work in this way.

A politics of human rights must seek power over the real conditions of enjoyment of formal entitlements. What a global politics of human rights will look like will follow from prior domestic experiences in developing contestatory programs. When a transatlantic progressive movement coalesced in the nineteenth century to challenge the misery of unregulated capitalism, it realized that invoking formal rights was insufficient—especially since the defenders of unregulated capitalism also commonly appealed to natural rights, such as the sanctity of the property entitlement. So progressives deformalized rights, suggesting they were not absolute metaphysical principles but contingent tools of pragmatic social organization.[5] The same move needs to happen at the global level now.

A politics of human rights will move away from framing norms individualistically and will cease to privilege political and civil liberties. In the same vein, and for the sake of targeting the world's worst miseries, human rights must move in the same direction as prior domestic progressives did. Just as they deformalized rights, they attacked the individualist character of rights for the sake

---

5. See, for example, Barbara H. Fried, *The Progressive Assault on Laissez Faire: Robert Hale and the First Law and Economics Movement* (Cambridge, MA, 1998).

of the common good or social solidarity, and insisted that the real conditions for the enjoyment of any rights are to be sought not simply in the possession of personal security but also in the entitlement to economic welfare.

Some movements—like Marxism—moved away from individualism and indeed rights altogether, but a politics of human rights will not do so. Yet it will have to move far from the classic concerns of the human rights movement since the 1970s, based as it has been on the campaign for political and civil rights against the totalitarian and authoritarian state (and now, most frequently, the postcolonial state). While it should not totally abandon its concern with evil states, it will need to make what has been an obsession a peripheral element in a larger campaign. Ultimately, it should engage in the programmatic concern with designing good states, for the sake of global economic welfare.

One might fairly ask what the incentive is to transform human rights in this way. The answer, I think, is that if the human rights movement does not offer a more realistic and politicized utopia, something else will take its place.

The geopolitical situation is changing rapidly. Human rights as depoliticized moral norms ascended far and fast in a particular world-historical situation, between the bipolar era of the Cold War and the multipolar era that is surely coming. In the immediate aftermath of the Cold War, before 9/11 intervened, Europeans flirted with the idea that American power needed to be balanced. Today, most people think that China will become the agent of balance.

A return to a geopolitics of contest inevitably brings about a world in which appealing to moral norms will no longer seem paramount. Human rights can retain their current prominence by becoming an open language of partisanship, so that other realists, for whom universalist justice is at best a secondary concern, do not hold the field.

But history also teaches us that partisanship is bittersweet. Human rights will descend into the world as a language of contest and struggle, but the other side will no longer be forced to defer to them as binding—a morality above politics. The other side may also offer its own interpretations of rights. We are fast departing from a world in which human rights became prominent, precisely because they seemed an alternative to contest and struggle, a pure utopia where others failed. Some people will view the descent of human rights into programmatic contest as too high a cost for relevance. But if the alternative is irrelevance, it is a small price to pay.

ACKNOWLEDGMENTS

With one exception, the chapters of this book originally appeared in the *Nation*, on the following dates respectively: Chapter 1, April 16, 2007; Chapter 2, November 4, 2013; Chapter 3, October 13, 2008; Chapter 4, March 19, 2012; Chapter 5, September 6, 2010; Chapter 7, February 25, 2013; Chapter 8, October 3, 2011. All are reprinted with permission of the magazine. Adam Shatz commissioned the first of these, which launched me in the field; but I owe by far most of my thanks for this book to John Palattella, who as literary editor of the *Nation* oversaw the other chapters from invitation to finalization. His talents as an editor and intellectual are full to the brim. These essays appear essentially verbatim, with only a few minor changes here and there.

The exception is Chapter 6, which originated as a talk at a conference on September 7, 2012 at the Graduate Center of the City of New York organized by Sarah Danielsson, to whom (along with her co-conspirator and my good friend Dirk Moses) I am likewise grateful. The epilogue, meanwhile, previously appeared (in somewhat different form) as an art catalogue essay in Katerina Gregos and Elena Sorokina, eds, *Newtopia:*

The State of Human Rights (Mechelen, 2012). These origins account for the informality of both pieces, but in compensation they point towards my current research and writing much more clearly. Lastly, thanks to Katrine Bregengaard for the first book epigraph.

It is owing to the generosity of Sebastian Budgen and Jacob Stevens that these materials appear as a book. Mark Martin and Lorna Scott Fox helpfully edited the text. Alisa Berger makes everything I do possible, while Lily and Madeleine Moyn—and most recently Sasha, my newborn niece—have taught me why our uses of the past must serve a better future.

INDEX